MAKE YOUR OWN LUNCH

How to Live an Epically Epic Life
through Work, Travel, Wonder, and (Maybe) College

Ryan Porter

Published by Sourcebooks, Inc.
P.O. Box 4410, Naperville, Illinois 60567-4410
(630) 961-3900
Fax: (630) 961-2168
www.sourcebooks.com

Library of Congress Cataloging-in-Publication Data is on file with the publisher.

Printed and bound in the United States of America.

VP 10 9 8 7 6 5 4 3 2 1

For Seiko

My life with you is the most epic life I could imagine.

Thank you.

Step 5: Chocolate-Covered Everything: Reap the Rewards of Hard Work, Realized Dreams, and All Things Sweet 189

Big-Ups & Shout-Outs 210

Resources & Tools 213

How to Contact Me 215

About Ryan 216

STEP 1

SETTING THE TABLE

IT'S LUNCHTIME! AN INTRODUCTION

Time to set the table (a.k.a. what's this book all about).

→ "When I yell, 'Paddle!' look straight ahead and paddle as hard as those pale, skinny arms can paddle!"

It was week two of my four-week trip to Hawaii and Japan. I was hanging out on the north shore of Oahu (the surfing capital of the world), taking surf lessons from a fifty-five-year-old surfing veteran.

My surfing instructor was yelling at me as I waited, lying on my surfboard, in ridiculous anticipation of my first wave. The sun was beating down on my neck, waves were crashing all around me, and I was beginning to get nervous.

"Remember, be patient. Whatever you do, watch out for the pearl!"

Before I had the time to remember that *the pearl* was surfer slang for a face-plant, my instructor was yelling, "Now! Paddle!"

And with that, I began paddling as hard as my pale, skinny arms could paddle. My adrenaline was pumping as hard as the water under my board, and as the wave began to break, it picked me up and carried me toward the shore. I waited, even though I felt the urge to stand up. My surfing instructor had specifically told me that when you feel the urge to stand up, paddle three more times and *then* get up.

One…two…three…

I quickly slid my hands to the sides of the board, planted my feet, and stood up. I threw my arms out to my sides for balance, and miraculously, I was surfing. I'm sure I looked ridiculous, and maybe a little out of place, but I couldn't have cared less. It felt awesome. I looked down at the wave then up at the beach. I couldn't believe it—I was actually surfing.

In high school, I couldn't have imagined that I would be doing what I do now. Traveling across North America talking to teens about how they too can do the things they want. I never thought I would write a book. I never pictured myself traveling around the world, camping on volcanoes in Guatemala, wearing samurai armor in Japan, surfing in Hawaii, or scuba diving in Honduras. My teachers and counselors never talked about other options.

They never guided with phrases like "be patient" or said anything about taking the time to figure things out. I was told there were three options: go to a four-year college, go to community college, or get a job. I wasn't confident that any of those options was right for me at the time, so I took another route. I decided to *make my own lunch*.

I'll explain what it means to "make your own lunch" in just a bit. In fact, the whole book is about exactly that. But what I mean in a nutshell is, we spend a ton of our young-adult lives being told what we *need* to survive and thrive. We're told what our success should look like (and what we should look like) and how we *should* go get it. And a lot of us end up eating it up and swallowing it even if it doesn't taste good going down.

Make Your Own Lunch is for you if any of the following apply:

- You are not sure if college is right for you.
- You know exactly what you want, but it doesn't include college and your next steps aren't clear.
- You have questions about school or what to do when you graduate.
- You don't know where to start your next adventure.
- You want to meet people who took career paths your counselors and teachers didn't talk about.
- You dream about traveling the world and exploring far-off places.
- You want to have fun and excitement in your life.
- You have trouble making decisions.
- You want to make changes to your school, your community, or the world.
- You want to start your own business.
- You're sick of staying at home talking to stuffed animals on weekends.
- You want to learn another language.

- You want a better relationship with your friends, family, or boyfriend or girlfriend.
- You hear that you can do anything, but you don't know what that means.
- You dream about living the life you want.
- You want freedom.
- You keep hearing people tell you that your dreams aren't realistic.
- You want success.
- You know there's a way to have what you want but don't know how to get it.
- You want a job or career you love.
- You want to study things you are passionate about.
- You don't know how to find your passion.
- You don't know what you want.
- You don't know where to go or what to do.
- You don't want to live like most of the people you know.
- You don't know who you are or who you could be.

Make Your Own Lunch is for *you*.

"What do you want to be when you grow up?"

That question haunted me for the first twenty-three years of my life. It started in kindergarten as a fun game of imagination, and by the end of high school, it had evolved into a giant monster breathing fire down my neck. High school finished and I still had no idea what I was going to be, so I took some time off to search for an answer. The quest to answer that question brought me to Japan, Hawaii, Slovakia, France, Honduras, Guatemala, Austria, Las Vegas, and more.

I'd love to act like my journey was all part of some master plan that I had carefully and meticulously crafted, mapping it out years in advance, but honestly, I had no idea what I was doing half of the time. The other half of the time, I was just doing what I was drawn to and what I thought would be best for me (and the most fun).

Somehow, while looking for the answer to the question, "What do you want to be when you grow up?" I realized the question was wrong. Wrong because there isn't only *one* thing you can do with your life. Wrong because it makes it sound like there's a direct path from A to B, when really there are a bunch of paths, side adventures, and detours. Wrong because it puts so much pressure on young people to "figure it out" immediately.

Once I started searching, I started uncovering new questions and a ton of really exciting answers. I began realizing that you really never have to have it *all* figured out. The next step is what's most important now, and it's fine if beyond that is a bit of a question mark.

I wrote this book so you don't have to waste time trying to answer ridiculous questions like, "What do you want to be when you grow up?" or "How much wood could a woodchuck chuck if a woodchuck could chuck wood?"

I wanted you to know that it's perfectly OK and perfectly normal to *not* know the answer to either of those questions. It's OK to take some time to figure yourself out and explore the many different paths that will lead you to the answers you're looking for.

WE SPEND A TON OF OUR YOUNG-ADULT LIVES BEING TOLD WHAT WE *NEED* TO SURVIVE AND THRIVE. WE'RE TOLD WHAT OUR SUCCESS SHOULD LOOK LIKE (AND WHAT WE SHOULD LOOK LIKE) AND HOW WE *SHOULD* GO GET IT. AND A LOT OF US END UP EATING IT UP AND SWALLOWING IT.

IT'S OK TO TAKE SOME TIME TO FIGURE YOURSELF OUT AND EXPLORE THE MANY DIFFERENT PATHS THAT WILL LEAD YOU TO THE ANSWERS YOU'RE LOOKING FOR.

This book was written over six years from various planes, trains, cars, hotel rooms, hostels, and the occasional jungle. Sometimes I wrote it on my office computer, other times on my laptop, and a few times with actual pen and paper. My goal was never to give you a specific plan, or *347 Strategies for Success in Career, Education, and Life*, because for some people there could be a bunch of steps, and for others there are just a few to reach their desired destination.

You'll figure out the steps you need to take. You'll come up with your own plan to make it happen. And you'll develop your own *strategies for career, education, and life success*.

Some parts of this book are really short; others are a bit longer. Take your time, read the stories, and while reading, write down any ideas or inspiration you might have. If while you're reading, you feel inspired to do something, call somebody, go somewhere, or build something, do it. This book isn't going anywhere...unless you left it on the subway, in which case, it is now a pillow for a tired backpacker.

Last, thank you for reading this. From this point, you begin (or continue) building your own epic life through experience, work, travel, wonder, and (maybe) college. Right now. It's go time.

—RYAN P.

2

MAKE YOUR OWN LUNCH

How to live an epic life and other helpful hints.

WHY ARE YOU PUTTING UP WITH STUFF YOU HATE?
IF THERE'S SOMETHING YOU DON'T LIKE, CHANGE IT. 'NUF SAID.

→ There were three construction workers named Simon, Andrew, and Bob. These three friends worked together as part of a construction crew building a skyscraper in the downtown area of a major city. One day, the crew's lunch bell rang and the three friends went to the top of the unfinished skyscraper to eat.

As they sat on the edge of the rooftop with their feet hanging hundreds of feet above the ground, Simon opened his lunch box, looked in disgust at his two friends, and shouted in frustration.

"A ham sandwich again! I get ham every day of the week, and I'm sick of it! If I get a ham sandwich one more day, I swear I'm going to jump off this building." Andrew and Bob laughed. Andrew put his lunch box on his lap and opened the latches on the front. When he flipped the lid open and saw what was inside, he shouted in disbelief.

"A turkey sandwich again! You've got to be kidding me. I get turkey every day of the week, and I've had enough! If I get a turkey sandwich one more day, I swear I will jump from this building!"

Bob was the only one laughing now. He opened his lunch box and pulled out his sandwich. Disappointed with what he had in his hands, he shouted in anger.

"A peanut butter sandwich again! This is getting ridiculous! I get peanut butter every day, and I'm sick of it! If I get peanut butter one more day, I swear *I'm* going to jump off this building!"

None of them was laughing now.

They were all extremely hungry, so they finished their lunches without talking and went back to work.

The next day, the three workers, as they had done the day before, sat down at the top of the skyscraper for their lunch break. They ate in the same spot as the day before, with their feet dangling high above the street. Simon got his lunch box from his work bag, opened it, and pulled out his sandwich. He erupted in anger.

"Can you guys believe this? A ham sandwich again! I am so sick of eating this every day! I told you guys how much I hate ham!" Simon slammed his sandwich down with fury and jumped from the building, plunging to his death.

Unfazed by what had just happened, Andrew opened his lunch box. He turned to Bob, and at the top of his lungs, he screamed, "Is this a joke? A turkey sandwich again? I get turkey every day and am so sick and tired of it. I have had enough!" He threw his sandwich down on the platform, stomped on it, and jumped from the building, falling to the street below.

Bob nervously opened his lunch box and slowly took his sandwich out. He separated the two slices of bread to reveal what was in the middle. In absolute frustration, he threw the sandwich to the platform and began jumping on it. As he jumped on his lunch, he yelled to the sky, "Why me? Why me? Why me? A peanut butter sandwich again? I can't believe this. I get this every day and can't take it anymore!" He didn't hesitate as he threw himself over the edge of the building.

A few days later, Simon, Andrew, and Bob's wives held a funeral for them. When the funeral was over, they met to console one another. Simon's wife spoke first. Through her tears and sniffling, she mumbled, "I…I…I don't understand. If Simon wanted something other than a ham sandwich, he should've asked me. I would've made him something different, but he never asked."

Andrew's wife put her arm around Simon's wife and agreed.

"I don't get it either. If Andrew was so sick of turkey sandwiches, why didn't he say something? I would've made him something different, but he never asked. I feel terrible!"

Bob's wife, clearly distraught, spoke next. "I don't understand. Bob made his own lunch."

[This is where you laugh.]

I'm not sure if this story is real or not. Actually, I'm still trying to figure out if the tooth fairy is real. I swear I saw her once. She was beautiful. #truestory

I bet I know what you're thinking though. *What an idiot* (not me or the tooth fairy, but Bob). *What's wrong with Bob? He has to be the stupidest person in this universe. Why would he make a lunch every day that he absolutely hated? Even crazier is why would he complain about it when he was the one making it?*

Who would do that?

You would.

Wait. Don't hit me!

The truth is, *you* are Bob (even if you're not a guy or your name isn't Robert).

Relax. Before you get angry and burn this book, we are *all* Bob sometimes. It's as natural as thick-framed glasses on a hipster (please note: I am wearing thick-framed glasses as I type this, so I'm not knocking it).

I'm positive you have spent time being upset about something like the weather or your weight or your relationship with someone in your family or that weird smell coming from your closet. Maybe you've complained that you have bad luck or that you have no idea what to do after high school. You're fed up that you can't stay focused. You can't get a boyfriend or girlfriend (or any kind of friend for that matter), and even your imaginary friends changed their relationship status to "It's complicated" on Facebook.

You may not always complain out loud, but in quiet moments by yourself, I'm sure you have had thoughts similar to these at least once or twice in your lifetime.

If you are anything like the average person, a day rarely goes by without complaining about something you aren't happy with or complaining about *something* in your life. Don't believe me? Look at your social media news feeds. Everybody is complaining about something.

Am I right? Don't answer out loud, especially if someone else is in the room. That's just weird. People will tweet about you. #thatawkwardmomentwhen

If I asked you to write down all of the things that aren't right, or that you aren't happy with, or that you want to change in your life, how long do you think you would be writing for? Five minutes? Ten minutes? An hour? A day?

Don't get me wrong. I'm not assuming that you just sit around all day complaining about your life and how bad things are. But I'm sure you would love to see some things change.

Don't worry. You're not alone. There are Bobs everywhere. We all spend time every day fed up, confused, or complaining about things in our lives that we have the power to change.

You, like Bob, *make your own lunch*! You decide what to do, when to do it, how

IF YOU ARE ANYTHING LIKE THE AVERAGE PERSON, A DAY RARELY GOES BY WITHOUT COMPLAINING ABOUT SOMETHING YOU AREN'T HAPPY WITH OR COMPLAINING ABOUT *SOMETHING* IN YOUR LIFE.

to do it, and most important, how you think and feel about it. And just like Bob, you get to do this every day.

Every day, you wake up with a ton of decisions to make. Some of them are as simple as deciding which pair of Hello Kitty socks match your outfit the best. Other decisions are slightly more difficult. Like deciding about going to that school you've always dreamed about, or getting that job you've always wanted, or taking a six-month surfing tour around the world. Or all three.

Or something completely different that's unique to you and you alone.

So yeah, we are all like Bob sometimes, but a lot of people spend a lot of time being like Simon and Andrew. Let's take a look, shall we?

Simon and Andrew

I think you'd agree with me that letting somebody else make decisions for you is never a good call. Oh, and if you need some kind of reminder, go back and look at awkward old family photos when your parents dressed you. Yeah. That's what I thought. Something tells me you didn't decide that the *entire* family should wear the matching kitten sweaters.

Simon and Andrew were a lot like that poorly dressed younger version of you. They were letting somebody else (a.k.a. their wives) make their lunches, and they spent every day complaining about it. They represent a large group of people who let other people make decisions for them. For some, it might be their parents; for others, it might be their boyfriends, girlfriends, friends, or teachers.

A few years ago, I spent some time filming a short low-budget, low-quality documentary about how college students choose their schools, their programs of study, and their courses. I thought I was going to hear stories of people following dreams and pursuing passions. Instead, I heard countless stories of students making decisions based on what their parents had told them or what their school counselors had suggested. Other students told me they did whatever their friends were doing.

It was really surprising.

Do you want to know how many of these people were happy with their decisions? About 30 percent said they were glad they listened to the advice they were given, and only *half* of that 30 percent were actually happy with their decision. The rest said they wished they had taken more time to figure out what really would have been best for them.

Simon and Andrew don't just represent the people who let others choose for them. They are the people who let others influence how they dress, what kind of music they listen to, how to act, how to feel, what to do on the weekend, who to be friends with, whether they should drink alcohol or take drugs, whether and when they should have sex, or even what to do in their spare time.

The Simons and Andrews of the world let others make decisions for them and then spend a lot of time complaining about it. The Simons and Andrews are the ones who usually live with regret and disappointment. They usually respond to people with statements like, "It's not my fault. _____ made me do it!"

When asked about their dreams and goals, they will probably tell you something like, "I wanted to do _____, but because of _____, I wasn't able to do it, so it isn't my fault."

People like Simon and Andrew will never be happy. They may experience short-term happiness because they feel accepted by the ones making decisions for them, but they will almost always end up miserable, full of regret, and wearing a really ugly denim vest with a giant unicorn on the back.

The Simons and Andrews of the world go through life forfeiting responsibility for their decisions. They would have been on time, but the *bus* was late. They would have gone for a run, but they were too *tired* (probably from staying up too late watching *The Bachelor*, *Teen Mom*, reruns of *The Hills*, or weird infomercials, or playing Xbox live). They *meant* to buy a birthday present, but the mall closed at 5 p.m. They want to be healthy, but their mom and dad are overweight, so it's in *their blood* to be overweight and unhealthy.

The Simons and Andrews of the world always claim to be victims, when in reality they could have taken an earlier bus, they could have gone to bed earlier the night before, they could have bought a birthday present a few days before Saturday. They could've read the directions on the box before trying to bleach their eyebrows. They could decide to work out and commit to being healthy regardless of the condition their parents are in. They could decide to change just about anything, but they don't because it's much easier to blame others for being miserable.

Simon and Andrew are lame. Sorry, Mr. Cowell and President Jackson. No offense.

If you are being a Simon or an Andrew, stop it! Take back control and start doing things *you* want to do. Go the places *you* want to go. Take the unicorn vest off and wear the clothes *you* want to wear. Hang out with the people *you* want to hang out with. Stop wasting time and be the person *you* want to be!

Bob

It's time we talked a little more about Bob, but first, can we just take a minute to nod our heads and agree that people hate complainers as much as they hate spam emails and trolls.

PEOPLE LIKE SIMON AND ANDREW WILL NEVER BE HAPPY. THEY MAY EXPERIENCE SHORT-TERM HAPPINESS BECAUSE THEY FEEL ACCEPTED BY THE ONES MAKING DECISIONS FOR THEM, BUT THEY WILL ALMOST ALWAYS END UP MISERABLE, FULL OF REGRET, AND WEARING A REALLY UGLY DENIM VEST WITH A GIANT UNICORN ON THE BACK.

WHETHER YOU LIKE IT OR NOT, *YOU* ARE THE REASON *YOU* ARE WHO YOU ARE RIGHT NOW. IF YOU LIKE THAT PERSON, AWESOME. IF YOU DON'T, DON'T SWEAT IT! YOU CAN DECIDE TO CHANGE FROM HERE ON OUT.

Lucky for you, you aren't a complainer. I like you. I wish I could say the same for Bob.

I have told the make-your-own-lunch joke to hundreds of thousands of students, and I have yet to have a group not laugh and not make fun of Bob in some way.

The sad thing is that there are more Bobs on this earth than any other group of people. The Bobs of this world spend a ton of time complaining about stuff they could change if they weren't so lazy! They are quick to complain, but they never do anything to change the things they are complaining about.

I bet you can name fifteen people like this off the top of your head. They are the people who do the same things over and over again and expect something different to happen. They have the same conversations all the time, and they probably spend the majority of the time complaining about something.

"I still don't have a good job." But they get up and go to the same job every day.

"I don't have any money." But they use their credit card to buy their 427th pair of Lacoste sunglasses.

"I keep gaining weight." But they eat deep-fried chocolate bars. (Yes, these exist. My brother suffered third-degree burns trying to make them.)

"I didn't make the team again!" But they roll over in bed and press "snooze" on their alarm.

"I failed another test." But they watch another rerun of *The Simpsons* instead of studying.

"My boyfriend is being a jerk." But they stay with him.

"I hate the way my parents are treating me!" But they break their curfew for the third weekend in a row.

"I am sick and tired of _____ every day!"

If you find yourself saying this kind of stuff every day, do me a huge favor and punch yourself in the throat. That way you won't be able to talk for a while.

OK, I actually don't condone violence, but the fact is, we don't want to hear it anymore.

Bobs spend too much time complaining about their lives, jobs, schools, communities, and relationships without ever trying to change them.

Do I really need to type it again?

Fine, I will: *You* make your own lunch!

Whether you like it or not, *you* are the reason *you* are who you are right now. If you like that person, awesome. If you don't, don't sweat it! You can decide to change from here on out.

I do need to mention one thing before we move on. There are certain situations you have no control over, things like being a victim of violence, war, sexual abuse, death, natural disasters, and divorce, and a *bunch* of other situations. Those things are completely out of your hands. Please, don't *ever* blame yourself for those situations. Please.

But as bad as those things are and as much pain, hurt, and sadness as they cause, you can choose to move on, to get help, to feel better, to speak out against those things, and to help others in the same situation. More important, you get to choose how to feel and what to think about that stuff. You have that kind of power.

Decide now to not let those things hold you back. Decide to move forward and become the exact person living the exact, incredible life that you want.

Decide to stop complaining about the things you can actually change, and decide to start making those changes.

The world has way too many Bobs in it.

Don't be one of them.

3

MY LUNCH STORY

A little background on making your own lunch through trial and error...my trial and error.

EVERYBODY HAS A STORY. HERE'S MINE.
RATED PG SO THE WHOLE FAMILY CAN ENJOY.
YOU'RE WELCOME.

Growing up, I was a "regular" dude (and no, this had nothing to do with probiotic yogurt or fiber). I came from a family of five kids. Yes, that's right. I said five kids. I have three brothers and one sister.

I wasn't a troublemaker, but I somehow always seemed to get in trouble. I wasn't a bad kid. I just liked excitement and couldn't stand being bored. And sometimes this may or may not have involved spray-painting our local community center while it was being built and being brought home by the police at age eight.

I had great grades all through school and was constantly doing things differently than what most people would call "the norm." Unless, of course, there are a lot of other people who bypassed running the traditional lemonade stand to make some PlayStation game money by catching fish from a river to start the neighborhood's first, and last, summer fish stand. Did I mention it was a very hot summer day?

I figured out early in life that I could make my own decisions. I learned that sometimes it worked out great and I made fantastic decisions, but other times things didn't work out as I had planned.

Here's a list of some of my decisions:

1. Not talking until I was three years old, which resulted in many visits to specialists and lots of worry from my parents, who were wondering if I was going to be "normal."
2. The first five years of my life, the dress code was "clothing optional." Anywhere. Anytime.

3. At age five, I raced a kid riding a bike while I was on foot. I slipped and fell, and then I was run over by the bike, which broke my leg.

4. At eight, I decided to say no to the girl who asked me if I would be her boyfriend. This resulted in my *first* face slap from a female.

5. At nine, I decided a pink dress shirt, denim vest, and cutoff leather gloves were cool—a decision I will never make again.

6. At thirteen, I decided to create my own public holiday with three friends: Fire Day.

7. At thirteen, I also decided that my basketball team was NBA bound. One win, twelve losses later, I decided it should have been a team decision.

8. At sixteen, I decided to mock a Shania Twain (country songstress) look-alike until she actually beat me up. #fail

9. At seventeen, I played the fainting game. After a severe concussion, giant gash across my face, and blood leaking into my eyeball, I decided we should have played road hockey instead.

10. At eighteen, I said "no to the flow" and didn't go to college after I graduated. I needed time to figure myself out.

11. At nineteen, I went to college and studied business and marketing. I learned later that I should've taken more time to figure this decision out.

12. At twenty, I bought the most luxurious car I could afford at the time. A 1983 Volkswagen Rabbit. Price: $500.

13. At twenty and a half, I decided that luxury cars start when you turn the key and don't have a football-sized rust hole in the hood. I decided the Rabbit wasn't luxury after all.

14. At twenty-one, I dropped out of college, moved out of my parents' home, and spent all of my savings and student loans on pointless partying, Mr. Noodles, and pizza.

After this point in life decisions can become a bit more serious, scary, and difficult to make.

At twenty-one, I felt like I went from enjoying my youth where decisions barely had an impact on my day to getting a little older and encountering decisions that could potentially affect the rest of my life. I mean, I went from deciding between "truth or dare" to "should I get a credit card or take out a student loan?"

During my second year of college, I found my classes boring. The school track I thought was right for me wasn't as exciting as I had hoped, so I dropped out of school. My parents weren't exactly thrilled. I moved into my friend's basement in

AFTER THIS POINT IN LIFE DECISIONS CAN BECOME A BIT MORE SERIOUS, SCARY, AND DIFFICULT TO MAKE.

a town outside of Toronto, Canada. The house was near the university my friends were attending, and I thought this was an awesome opportunity to live the university party life without actually going to university. This is what is referred to in the *Oxford English Dictionary* as "The Perfect Plan." #theperfectplan

I thought this idea was *so* great that I could afford to quit my job as the frozen-food section manager at our local grocery store, Tom's No Frills, and bank my entire future on the plan.

I lived with my friend and his roommates for about three months with no job, scraping by on ramen noodles and pickled banana peppers. I had spent all of my student loans and drained my savings account, and I wasn't sure how I would pay my already-late rent, when one random Sunday, my mom, who just happens to be a career counselor, decided to pay me a surprise visit and treat me to lunch.

Imagine what it was like for her, a career counselor, having a son who was unemployed, not in school, and had no idea what he wanted to do with his life. That's like Chuck Norris's son not being able to grow a beard by age thirteen. The shame would be unbearable.

When we got to the restaurant, she didn't even let thirty seconds pass before she asked me a question. Not just *a* question but *the* question—the very question I had been avoiding for the previous couple of years: "Ryan, what are you doing with your life?"

Knowing I couldn't tell her that I was thinking about becoming a professional thumb wrestler, I remember thinking to myself, "If only *I* knew."

I had tried so hard not to think about that question. I had stuffed it into the boxes with my college textbooks and elementary school love letters (all two of them) and had thrown it into the corner of a room in my parents' house, where I no longer lived.

I thought about the question for a minute and came up with the smoothest answer I could think of at that time: "Mom, don't worry about it. I'm just going with the flow."

Apparently, this wasn't the answer she was hoping for, and I quickly realized this "lunch chat" was going to be the second most uncomfortable conversation I would have with a parent. I am sure you can guess what other conversation has the number-one spot.

My mom went on to tell me how worried she was about me. She told me all of the things she thought I should be, and could be, doing, and I did everything in my power to make her stop trying to counsel me and let me eat my chicken wrap in peace.

You've probably had a similar conversation at some point with a parent, friend, relative, or teacher. Not so fun, eh?

Finally, just when I thought I couldn't handle another minute of the lecture, our bill came. I reached into my empty pockets and acted like I was going to pay (knowing my mom wouldn't let me). My mom reached across the table, took the bill, put some cash on top of it, and stood up to leave.

We grabbed our coats, and as we were about to get into the family minivan, she reached into her pocket and handed me an envelope with some cash in it. I pretended I didn't need it and made a few weak attempts to refuse, but I eventually put it in my coat pocket, knowing my rent was past due.

After an awkward drive back to my basement apartment, it was time to say good-bye. As a final attempt to break the uncomfortable silence, my mom jokingly said, "Well, if you really have no idea what to do, you could just move to Japan and teach English or something."

We both laughed hysterically at the ridiculous thought.

Before I could open the door to the house, I heard those words in my head again, "...Japan."

Being somebody who decided when I was young to always opt for the adventurous path, once inside the house, I ran straight into my friend's room, jumped on the Internet, and searched "teach English in Japan."

That decision changed my life.

Within minutes, I had found a company that hired English teachers out of Toronto to send to Japan. I reviewed my résumé to make sure it sounded like I was a good candidate for the job and sent it to the company that same afternoon. I didn't tell anyone about what I had done because I assumed there was no chance they would hire me to teach English in Japan. I was a college dropout whose only work experience was stocking frozen okra in a grocery store.

Little did I know.

Two days later, the phone rang. The company I sent my résumé to wanted to interview me for a teaching position in Japan. I couldn't believe it! There was a chance I could move to Japan. I was excited. I was nervous. I was confused, and then...I was scared. How was I going to tell my mom that her joke gave me the idea to move to Japan?

I picked up the phone and called my mom.

"Hey, Mom, I just thought I would let you know I have a job interview this week."

My mom was so excited. "That's great, Ryan. Which company called you back?"
I hesitated and then answered, "Well, it's a company that hires English teachers to teach in Japan."

"Ryan, I was joking about that!"

Silence…sniffles…silence.

She spoke through her tears. Reading from the *Book of Mom*, she said, "That's great. I am so excited for you."

A few days later, I jumped on the subway and headed to downtown Toronto, wearing my dad's suit (which was approximately nineteen times too big for me) for the job interview.

The interview lasted four hours. I left the company office that day feeling supremely confident that there was no way I would ever get the job and that maybe *I* needed English lessons. I completely bombed the interview, and to top it all off, I looked absolutely ridiculous wearing my dad's pin-striped suit!

A week later, I ran out of money and had to move back to my parents' house. Defeated and feeling horrible about myself, I went back to the grocery store I used to work at and asked the owner if I could work for him again. He agreed to let me return, but my old manager position was filled, and I would have to go back to being a grocery boy, stocking shelves and making less money than I had been before.

One afternoon not too long after the interview, while sitting in my parents' kitchen eating peanut butter with a spoon, the phone rang. I picked it up, because that's what you do when a phone rings.

I said hello and then heard a woman ask, "May I speak to Ryan Porter, please?" She told me she was calling on behalf of the company that had interviewed me for the position in Japan. I assumed that this was the courtesy "Thanks for coming out, champ—better luck next year" phone call for the people who didn't get the job, but then I heard the words, "Your orientation package is in the mail and you should receive it in a few days. Fill out the required forms and send it back as soon as possible, because your contract begins in two months."

I was silent. I wasn't sure what this meant.

"Congratulations, Ryan. We are excited to have you join our company."

I was stunned. I got the job! I went storming into my parents' room. "Mom, Dad, I got the job! I'm moving to Japan!"

Silence…sniffles…silence.

This time, my dad stepped in and bailed my mom out so she didn't have to speak while crying, "They must've liked your suit!"

Things were about to get really crazy. I was going to Japan.

Do you want to know what it's like showing up in a country with no plan, no money, no idea how to speak the language, and no clue about its history, culture, or people? Keep reading, my friend. But before we get there, I need to ask you to do something.

Make one decision now. Make the decision right now to read this whole book. Read every chapter and question the things I write about. Figure out for yourself whether you think things in this book can help you. I promise you that as you read *Make Your Own Lunch* and question the ideas, you will learn more about yourself and see the power you have to change the things you're sick of. You'll see that it *is* realistic for you to live an epically epic life of epicness. You will see just how exciting it can be to make your own lunch.

MAKE ONE DECISION NOW. MAKE THE DECISION RIGHT NOW TO READ THIS WHOLE BOOK. READ EVERY CHAPTER AND QUESTION THE THINGS I WRITE ABOUT.

These aren't just random words I decided to throw together while taking a break from playing *Tiny Wings*. I live by the words on these pages, and I know how empowering and exciting it is to break free from the things people tell me I can and can't do and to live the life I want to live. My hope is that some of my experiences—epic fails and epic wins—can help you decide what you want and help you figure out how you'll get it.

So now you've read a little bit about my story, and as much as I like telling it to everybody and anybody who wants (or doesn't want) to hear it, it actually has a point: there's no set path for you.

You can decide to do the things that you really want to do. You can decide to travel the world. I travel as much as I can and still have a "real job."

You can decide to start a business or work for a company you are stoked about. You can live a life of freedom. You can be healthy. You can be successful. You can learn new skills. You can meet new people. You can be different from everybody in your family or circle of friends. You can live the exact life that you want to live.

You can *make your own lunch*.

Decision is all you have. It's also all you need. It's the most powerful thing on this planet. It's the only way you will ever get what you truly want.

You make your own lunch just like Dominic made his. (Don't know who Dominic is yet? Keep reading.) Your lunch—of course (a pun!)—is a simple analogy of your life, what you choose to do today, tomorrow, and beyond.

Some people learn this as teenagers and then use it their entire lives to live exactly how they want to, but many other people decide to take Bob's route. They decide never to change. They sit and settle for the crap they get every day, crap they hate, and they never do anything about it.

You will decide not to be Bob (no offense, Robert, Bob, or Bobby). You want more, you deserve more, and you are going to have more.

Now, let's head to the land of the rising sun.

DECISION IS ALL YOU HAVE. IT'S ALSO ALL YOU NEED. IT'S THE MOST POWERFUL THING ON THIS PLANET. IT'S THE ONLY WAY YOU WILL EVER GET WHAT YOU TRULY WANT.

4

BENTO BOX

Sometimes the greatest adventures come from the simplest decisions—like deciding to live *juuust* outside your comfort zone.

ORDER OFF THE MENU: TWO PIECES OF TEMPURA SHRIMP, A LITTLE BIT OF RICE, AND A WHOLE LOT OF RANDOMNESS.

When I landed in Tokyo in March 2004, I didn't know a single word of Japanese. I knew nothing about Japan, the culture, the history, or the people. I couldn't read a single character from any of the *three* Japanese alphabets, or understand even the most basic phrases, and honestly, I would've struggled to find it on a globe.

Most people would have taken months, or maybe even years, to make the decision I made that afternoon after speaking with my mom. I had no idea what that decision would lead to, but I was open for just about anything and looking to have a great adventure.

My teaching placement was at the company's branch in Shibuya Miyamasuzakashita.

Yup. That's what I thought.

When I first received the placement, I remember thinking, "Grrrrreat…a fishing village. I'm probably going to have to eat sushi every day and hand wash my kimono while drinking green tea with geisha."

All I knew about Japan was what I had seen in the movies. Samurai, geisha, robots, and vending machines that sell used underwear.

I arrived in Japan a little nervous, slightly excited, completely clueless, and wondering if my underwear would ever end up in a vending machine. I wasn't sure what I should be doing or how to get where I was supposed to be going. Lucky for me, my company had supplied me with instructions and a map of how to get to the office.

I ARRIVED IN JAPAN A LITTLE NERVOUS, SLIGHTLY EXCITED, COMPLETELY CLUELESS, AND WONDERING IF MY UNDERWEAR WOULD EVER END UP IN A VENDING MACHINE.

Using my handy map, I went from a bus to a train to another train on a separate train line and finally arrived at my destination. As I left the train station, I was surprised I didn't see any geisha or samurai. Instead, I found myself standing in the center of the busiest intersection in the world. Google "Shibuya" or "Shibuya Scramble Crossing" and check it out for yourself.

Here's a snapshot of Tokyo: there are more than thirteen million people in the heart of the city, and in the region, there are more than thirty million. The intersection I worked at had between one million and three million people crossing there every single day. Every time there was a green light, up to three thousand people would cross.

I'm from a place called Ajax in Ontario, Canada. (No relation to the toilet cleaner.) Our population, last time I checked, was ninety-one thousand. *Our* busiest intersection has eleven people, three dogs, and sometimes a raccoon crossing at it every day. Imagine how crazy it was going from Ajax to Tokyo.

Exactly.

One day, after living in Tokyo for a few months, I was preparing my most famous lesson, "How to Rob a Bank." That's right. I was being paid to teach students how to rob banks. The original lesson plan was called "How to Organize a

Party." I thought this was boring. Because of my limited experience committing crimes, I may or may not be responsible for every botched robbery in Japan since 2004. (I kid! I kid!)

I decided to put the lesson plan down and step out on our office balcony overlooking downtown Tokyo.

Across the street, the neon signs were flashing outside of a giant electronics store. Further down the road, there was a scramble crossing with people piling into the intersection from every side. People bowed as they spoke on the phone, even though the other person couldn't see them.

Music blared from every direction. The smell of delicious food was everywhere. People were screaming, "*Onegaishimasu!*" as they handed out packages of tissue with advertisements printed on them to passing pedestrians. Store clerks were shouting, "*Irasshaimase!*" every time their automatic doors slid open. Groups of office workers bowed as they thanked each other for their hard work, saying, "*Otsukaresama deshita.*"

I was feeling great. I was smiling. I couldn't believe that I was there, in the middle of Tokyo, seeing a different part of the world, by myself, doing something as fun as teaching English to some of the most incredible people I had ever met. But suddenly my feelings of happiness disappeared.

I started feeling a new emotion—anger.

"Why didn't anybody tell me I could do this? Why didn't my counselors in high school give me this option? Why weren't any of my friends aware that this was a possibility for work? Why didn't I know I could travel the world and do something I love and get *paid* for it?"

I felt completely and utterly ripped off. I felt let down by the people who were supposed to guide me to the career of my dreams and help me make the best decisions for my future. That's when I made a decision.

I decided to let other people know. To let them know that there's something out there for them, whether it's teaching English in Japan, or studying monkeys in Costa Rica, or preparing tax returns in Delaware. Maybe it's becoming a lawyer for a giant firm, or doing work for a nonprofit company helping senior citizens, or collecting books to send to children across the globe—or *all* of those things. Your life doesn't have to be some watered-down version—a compromised version—of the things you want.

Living in Japan, meeting people from all over the world, and hearing stories of the incredible things they had experienced—the places they had been, the jobs they had worked, the people they had met—helped me realize that it is possible to travel the globe, to find work that you love, and to live life on your own terms.

I STARTED FEELING A NEW EMOTION—ANGER. "WHY DIDN'T ANYBODY TELL ME I COULD DO THIS? WHY DIDN'T MY COUNSELORS IN HIGH SCHOOL GIVE ME THIS OPTION? WHY WEREN'T ANY OF MY FRIENDS AWARE THAT THIS WAS A POSSIBILITY FOR WORK? WHY DIDN'T I KNOW I COULD TRAVEL THE WORLD AND DO SOMETHING I LOVE AND GET *PAID* FOR IT?"

And it's possible to start now. You don't have to wait until you make a million dollars or get a PhD from Harvard. You can start right now, where you are, with what you have.

All your life, you may have been told, "You can do anything you set your mind to." *What?* Thanks for *nothing*, everybody.

The world has so many possibilities. So many, in fact, that often, you probably aren't even sure what you *want* to do. It can be so overwhelming, confusing, and — let's be honest — even scary at times.

A lot of the time, all you really need is somebody to point you in the right direction to get you on your way toward figuring out where you're going and what you're doing.

That's where I come in.

Moving to Japan was something that interested me (once I actually heard about it), and it sounded like it would be exciting and different than "the norm." It didn't take me long to make the decision to go. I also knew that if I went, I wouldn't be missing out on anything in Ajax. And besides, if I didn't like it, I could go home.

Having the option of going back home was never about having a plan B. It was about having different options along the same path. Options that would continue to move me closer to the stuff I wanted while having some epic adventures.

Was I scared when I left my home country? Of course! Was I nervous? Absolutely. I peed my pants three times on the airplane. Just kidding. Kind of.

People want you to think that making decisions is completely permanent. The entire time I was in high school, my teachers acted like the world would actually end if I didn't decide what I wanted to do with the rest of my life exactly three months before I graduated.

They made it sound like I had to make *one decision* that I would have to live with for the rest of my life. I think that's the biggest lie we've been fed all of our lives — that we need to choose one thing to do for the rest of our lives. It's bull crap (sorry, Mom — I had originally typed *puppy poop*, but it didn't have the same effect).

My philosophy is this: if there's something you want to do, do it! As long as it doesn't hurt someone physically and it's legal and ethical — that means no selling your kidney or your little cousin on eBay — then you need to do it. Keep in mind that every decision comes with a price tag called "consequence," and that is something you can't control (more on this later).

PEOPLE WANT YOU TO THINK THAT MAKING DECISIONS IS COMPLETELY PERMANENT. THE ENTIRE TIME I WAS IN HIGH SCHOOL, MY TEACHERS ACTED LIKE THE WORLD WOULD ACTUALLY END IF I DIDN'T DECIDE WHAT I WANTED TO DO WITH THE REST OF MY LIFE EXACTLY THREE MONTHS BEFORE I GRADUATED.

The good thing is that you can fix most decisions. If you don't know what to do after school, then decide to travel or work, or do something that will help you figure it out. Don't jump into college and go tens of thousands of dollars into debt because everyone else is. Decide to do what's right for you!

I MADE MY OWN LUNCH

DOMINIC

For Dominic, college always made sense. Despite spending much of his childhood moving around and living in places like Singapore and seeing great as well as terrible examples of education, he always got great grades and even skipped half a grade. Dominic *liked* school and was always excited about learning. College was always in his plans.

As Dominic neared his final semester of his senior year, however, he began really thinking about life after high school. He questioned whether it was right for him to go to college directly after high school.

One day, Dominic's mom approached him with an article from the *New York Times* about taking a "gap year" after high school. Although the newspaper made a gap year sound great, Dominic still believed that college was right for him and applied for college as he had always planned to.

But as a bit of an experiment, Dominic also applied for a gap-year program with an organization called City Year (www.cityyear.org).

He got accepted to the University of Chicago as he knew he would, but more surprising, he also got accepted to City Year.

After giving it a ton of thought and talking with some friends and family, Dominic chose to defer his first year of college and join City Year to work in inner-city schools in the West Side of Chicago.

His gap year was one of the most challenging and one of the most rewarding years of Dominic's life.

He spent eleven to twelve hours a day working with troubled youth, supporting the students, and keeping them current with their schoolwork. As he was working with the students, he began to realize that education is a lot like a sport or acting, and the more you practice it, the better you become.

He saw the importance of practical learning and learning beyond a textbook, and as his gap year came to an end, he realized how much he had changed. Although college was still in his plans, his opinion of college, formalized learning, and life after high school was completely transformed.

When I connected with Dominic, he talked about what it meant to spend an entire year out of his comfort zone. Not a day, not a weekend, but an entire *year* doing things that he had never done before.

Dominic is now a student at the University of Chicago, but he's also an intern at City Year, working with the organization in a different role and gaining a new perspective on life, school, and work.

I finished my chat with Dominic by asking him how things would've been different if he hadn't taken a gap year.

Dominic told me that he learned things that he couldn't have learned in a classroom, he learned to explore and step out of his comfort zone, but he also learned that in the end, college is right for him and the life he wants.

His final words about gap years for students: "Take a gap year…a *directed* gap year, not just a year of taking photos and hanging out. Take a year where you are giving, learning, and gaining experience, regardless of your postsecondary destination."

Dominic decided to try something new from the lunch menu, to try something that was a bit out of the ordinary and out of his comfort zone. He was rewarded with amazing experiences, extraordinary learning opportunities, and incredible lifelong friends.

Don't take over the family business because you feel pressured from your dad and your uncle Frank. (Everyone has an Uncle Frank. Even if his name's not Frank, you have one. It's a scientific fact. Look it up.)

Don't eliminate the idea of college because your school counselor told you that you can't handle it. And like Dominic learned, don't be afraid to push "pause" on your plan to try something new and get a better perspective on things.

Do what you feel is going to give you the best experiences and help you answer those difficult questions that life throws at you, like who are you? (Note: if you are looking at the tag on your underwear to find out, that's a problem—if it's not your name on them, that's an even bigger problem.)

These are some other difficult questions:

- What are you passionate about?
- What are you great at?
- What's the purpose of your life?
- What do you do that makes you feel great and empowered?

- How can you do the things you want?
- Where do you start?

These are questions you are going to have to ask and answer for yourself. I won't tell you what to do, but I can help start you down the path to answering those questions. I'm not telling you not to go to college. I'm encouraging you to explore your options to help figure out what's best for you and *your* future.

Japan, though maybe not right for you and the things you want, was something that helped me figure it out. You're going to have your own way of doing things, and you'll have your own decisions to make that will bring you to the awesomeness that's waiting for you.

Remember how Simon, Andrew, and Bob made decisions? Yeah. Don't be like them. Really. Stop it.

If you *can* stop it, then you're on the road to epicness—even if *epicness* isn't a real word.

I'M NOT TELLING YOU NOT TO GO TO COLLEGE. I'M ENCOURAGING YOU TO EXPLORE YOUR OPTIONS TO HELP FIGURE OUT WHAT'S BEST FOR YOU AND *YOUR* FUTURE.

STEP 2

COOKIN' IT UP

5

THE MAIN INGREDIENT: DECISION

Decision is the ultimate superfood.

DECISION IS THE ONLY WAY ANYONE HAS ACCOMPLISHED ANYTHING...EVER.

—RYAN PORTER (PSST...THAT'S ME.)

→ I remember watching a TV show about people who had survived catastrophes and near-death experiences—people who had lived through terrible natural disasters, plane crashes, animal attacks, car wrecks, boat accidents, and Oasis concerts.

I found myself amazed by their incredible stories. The video footage of exploding factories, avalanches, horrendous car crashes, and bear attacks made it hard not to be amazed by their survival and will to live. Each person told his or her story and was then interviewed about the experience. The survivors were asked the same questions, and every single one of them answered the question, "How were you able to survive?" with almost the same response.

"I *decided* not to give up."

"I *decided* I wouldn't die."

"I *decided* I would see my family again."

In these tragic situations, as they stared death in the face, sometimes with broken bones and serious injuries, at times unable to move or talk, each survivor recognized how powerful his or her decisions were.

Nobody answered that fate saved them. They didn't attribute their survival to karma, lucky numbers, destiny, horoscopes, or star alignment. They knew that their *decision* to live was stronger than the situations they experienced. Decision is what saved their lives.

Decision is the only way anyone has ever accomplished anything, ever. So if you haven't clued in yet, this book is basically about one thing: decision.

It's about deciding to create the exact life you want. It's about making the decision to stop blaming other people, bad luck, crappy karma, expired dairy products, strange fortune cookies, or fate, and deciding to take ownership of your world.

It's about taking into consideration and then politely ignoring what your parents, teachers, friends, horoscope, Magic 8 Ball, and psychic are telling you, if the direction they want you to go in and their expectations aren't right for you. You have the power to decide whatever you want. And by ignoring those other things, you need to realize that good or bad, happy or sad, you are responsible for you.

How you feel today is a decision. Happiness is a decision. Health is a decision. Success is a decision. Failure is a decision. Sadness is a decision. Living an unhealthy lifestyle is a decision. Almost everything you feel, think, and do is a decision.

Of course, as I mentioned before, there are certain situations you have no control over, like being taken hostage, being attacked, losing a loved one, being diagnosed with cancer, being falsely thrown in prison, or being cheated on. However, what you take from those situations, as tough as they are, is a decision.

How you learn from those things, how you grow from them, and how you let them affect your life is a decision. Even in the worst situations you could imagine, you always have a choice. You get to decide how you think and how you feel. Luckily, no one controls that but you.

Don't believe me? Walk into any Tim Hortons (for my Canadian homies) or Starbucks or McDonald's (for everyone else) on any given morning and watch the people in line. Everybody is in the exact same line, waiting to be served, yet some people decide to let little things drive them crazy.

You know the type of person I'm talking about. I'm talking about that one guy everyone wants to punch in the ear when he starts freaking out because they took more than twenty-seven seconds to make his Egg McMuffin and put *only* 7.16 sugars in his coffee.

Those people decide to spend their entire wait time complaining to anyone with ears. And when they are being served, they are completely rude and ignorant to the server, just to let the server know how long they waited.

How is it that other people stand in the same line, facing the same problem, but do it with a smile on their face? Is it because these people are better people? No, it's because these other people decided not to let a little line and wait time ruin their day. (Keep reading if you think you *can't* control your thoughts, feelings, and responses—even those slap-your-brother-in-the-back-of-the-head-without-thinking responses.)

EVEN IN THE WORST SITUATIONS YOU COULD IMAGINE, YOU ALWAYS HAVE A CHOICE. YOU GET TO DECIDE HOW YOU THINK AND HOW YOU FEEL. LUCKILY, NO ONE CONTROLS THAT BUT YOU.

It's time to start making some decisions.

Decide to create your future, not the one your parents have planned for you. Not the future in which brain-eating zombies invade the earth. Not the future your teachers keep telling you to prepare for. Not the future you *think* is right but the future you *want*.

→ A few years ago, I was speaking at a high school in Kansas. After I finished the *Make Your Own Lunch* presentation, a twelfth-grade girl approached me with a giant smile on her face.

"Ryan, thank you so much for speaking and sharing your stories, it was great."

"You're welcome."

The smile disappeared and she started to get a bit more serious. "Ryan, I have a huge problem…"

Uh-oh.

"I'm a straight-A student."

Huh?

"Wait, Ryan, it gets worse. I'm also captain of the volleyball team *and* student council president."

I was about as confused as I had ever been.

"Umm…Do you guys speak a different language down here? I'm from Canada and I know sometimes our English doesn't make sense, but I have no idea how any of those things are problems?"

"They're a problem because I want to be a *baker.*"

I smiled. "That's amazing! You know what you want to do after high school. You're ahead of the game."

Still not seeing the good in all of this, she told me, "Last week, I went to see my school counselor to talk about which college I should apply to. I told her I wasn't going to apply, but that I was going to go work in a bakery and get some experience."

Now I was genuinely curious. "What did she say?"

"She said, 'What a waste!…A smart, talented girl like you wasting your time making cupcakes?' Ryan, I couldn't believe it. All I want to do is bake. I want to see kids smile when they walk into my bakery, I want a bride and groom to cut the cake I made for them on their special day, and I want families to gather around my creations to create perfect memories."

As much as things didn't make sense when she started listing her problems, now they made sense.

People have expectations for you. There are people out there who believe that they know what's best for you and your future. And even though a lot of the time they have the best intentions, it's up to you to decide whether to listen to them or not. Your decisions enable you to move forward with confidence or to hold back with fear.

Your decisions shape who you are, where you'll go, and how you'll move forward. So, how do you start making decisions?

How about starting by really taking a look at the way you're feeling right now?

- How do you feel and think about your future?
- What kind of things do you see yourself doing?
- What kind of person do you want to become?
- What kind of advice are you getting, and how does it make you feel?

We'll tackle these questions in a bit more detail later, but for now, to understand how to make your own lunch, you can start by understanding this: **everything you are right now is because of your decisions up to this point.**

Even more important: **everything you will be in the future will be because of your decisions from today on.**

Ya dig?

I'm not writing this to stress you out or to make you feel bad or guilty about decisions you made (or haven't made) in the past. I'm writing this book so you can recognize that you have the power to change anything you want, whenever you want.

If you feel lost, you can find your way.

If you aren't getting the grades you want, you can change them.

If you are unhappy, you can decide to be happy.

If you smell like cat food, you can decide to shower.

How do I know? Because I've met thousands of people from all ends of this planet who are doing it. I've met rich people who are miserable, poor people who are happy, healthy people with complaints, and sick people with smiles on their faces. I've met high school students who've figured it out and college graduates who are completely lost.

EVERYTHING YOU ARE RIGHT NOW IS BECAUSE OF YOUR DECISIONS UP TO THIS POINT. EVEN MORE IMPORTANT: *EVERYTHING YOU WILL BE IN THE FUTURE WILL BE BECAUSE OF YOUR DECISIONS FROM TODAY ON.*

What separates these groups of people? You guessed it! *Decision.*

Is it all unicorns, double rainbows, and triple-frosting chocolate cupcakes? No. But when things do start to suck, you can decide to deal with it because you know you're working toward the awesome stuff you want.

And trust me, I'm not trying to oversimplify it and make decision making sound like a late-night infomercial. "In just *three* seconds, boom! You can have the life you want and enough tasty vegetable smoothies for your whole family."

Decision making can be tough. Making an informed decision can take time, research, and uncomfortable conversations.

For example, if you think that you want to take a year off after high school to backpack across Europe while building your web design portfolio before looking for a job or going to school, it might require you to really research the options, weigh the pros and cons, find other people who've done something similar, track down some mentors, and convince your parents that it's the best decision for you. It might involve mixed emotions, hurt feelings, and sleepless nights. But if you are constantly moving forward, learning, and making those decisions with your vision guiding you, armed with research and support, then managing some emotional ups-and-downs is definitely worth it.

You're on your own with the smoothies though.

Decision is the only way you will ever break free from the lunch box that people are trying to stuff you into. It's the only way you will get the ingredients you need to live the life you dream about.

So, what's your takeaway here? Decision is the main ingredient of *making your own lunch.* Your decisions are what set you apart from everyone else. Your decisions are what will allow you to do exactly what you want to do.

But remember, every decision has a consequence, good or bad. (Side note: make decisions. Just don't make decisions the way I made decisions while in Japan. Trust me.)

DECISION IS THE ONLY WAY YOU WILL EVER BREAK FREE FROM THE LUNCH BOX THAT PEOPLE ARE TRYING TO STUFF YOU INTO. IT'S THE ONLY WAY YOU WILL GET THE INGREDIENTS YOU NEED TO LIVE THE LIFE YOU DREAM ABOUT.

6

POINT, SMILE, & HOPE

How to know yourself enough to identify what you want without guessing, crossing fingers, wishing on falling stars, and other terrible ways of deciding your future!

GETTING EXACTLY WHAT YOU WANT IS A LOT MORE FUN THAN HOPING THAT ONE DAY YOU DISCOVER A CLOSET THAT TRANSPORTS YOU TO A MAGICAL KINGDOM FILLED WITH TALKING BOARS AND CENTAURS.

→ I spent my first three days in Tokyo at our main office with a group of people learning how to teach English to Japanese students. After the third day, we were ready to teach. To make our graduation official, the trainers brought the new employees to a Japanese restaurant to celebrate.

I was so stoked about this because up until that point, I had eaten nothing but KFC and McDonald's, and that's because Big Mac is still Big Mac in Japanese. Well, actually it's *biggu makku*, but close enough that people could understand what I was ordering.

When we were seated in the restaurant, the server came over and handed me my menu. I opened it up and immediately felt my stomach drop and sweat beginning to build in my armpits.

Not only was the menu written in Japanese but it had no pictures. And to make matters worse, not a single person in my group, including all three trainers, could read, speak, or understand Japanese. This was a bit confusing for me seeing as we were in *Japan*.

And the icing on the cake? Nobody in the restaurant spoke English.

One of my coworkers turned to me, panicking. "Ryan, can you read this?"

"Nope."

"Neither can I. Here, you order for me!" he said, as he handed me his menu.

I had to think fast. I had to develop a method of

ordering food in Japan. A method that was so ingenious I used it for the entire year I lived there.

The method is simple. I call it "point, smile, and hope."

Yup. That's right. It's as scientific as nuclear fusion and spontaneous combustion.

It works like this: you take a menu, point anywhere you like, smile to be polite, and then hope that you get something you can eat, that you have eaten before, or that you would consider eating.

OK, so it isn't exactly the algorithm Google uses to display search results for searching "is it impossible to lick your elbow," and it didn't always work out as planned, but I didn't know what else to do.

I looked around the restaurant and noticed that the other trainees were just as nervous. Two Australian girls in our group were so frustrated that they actually got up and left and went to McDonald's for a *biggu makku*. A bunch of other people with us refused to order anything and looked around in silence.

When it was my time to order, I simply pointed to a random place on the menu, smiled to be polite, and hoped I got something I could eat. The "point, smile, and hope" worked out great. Sometimes I would get things I loved or things that I learned to love. I would get things like fried chicken, salads, sushi, sandwiches, soup, or hamburgers.

Other times, I wasn't so lucky, and in those times "point, smile, and hope" brought me things like *basashi*. Oh, you don't know what that is? Let me help with the translation. *Basashi* is raw horse. Take it in for a second. Horse that is uncooked.

Another time, I sat down for dinner with my friend Toshi. Toshi is Japanese, so he reads, speaks, and understands Japanese. As the server came to our table, he asked if I needed help ordering. I refused.

"I've got this." I took a menu, held it up to the server, pointed, and smiled.

The server laughed at me.

The first indication that you are about to get something really weird is when the server laughs at you when you place your order.

She walked away, and I asked Toshi, "Dude, what did I just order?"

"*Shirako.*"

"That doesn't help me. I don't speak Japanese. What's *shirako*?"

Toshi burst out laughing. "I'm not telling."

The second indication that you are about to get something really weird is when your Japanese friend doesn't tell you what you've just ordered.

The server came back and put my dish down in front of me. As she placed it on the table, the dish jiggled like a gelatin mold. I asked Toshi one more time. "Can you please tell me what I am about to eat?"

"I am not sure how to say it in English." He pulled out an electronic dictionary and typed the word *shirako*.

With a giant smile on his face, he slid the dictionary across the table with the screen facing me, and said, "*Shirako? Shirako* is fish sperm."

That's right. Fish. Sperm.

Who knew?

My mind was filled with so many questions. Questions like, what the heck is that doing on a menu? How do they get it? And thanks to that thought, I had another: whose job is it to get it? Can you imagine career day at school for their kid? "My dad is the *shirako* guy." Yup.

So…I moved back to Canada.

OK. Not that day! I wasn't *that* disturbed by a little fish sperm. I finished my yearlong contract as a teacher a few months after the *shirako* incident and moved back to good ol' Ajax.

Since I've moved back to Canada, I've had the opportunity to work with hundreds of thousands of students, a ton of teachers, and many different organizations. I have come to realize that too many people take the same approach to their lives, relationships, school, and work as I did when ordering food in Japan.

When they have decisions to make, they simply point, smile, and hope it turns out all right. Or even worse, they approach their decisions like my coworkers did. They either get up and leave (don't do anything), or they let someone else decide for them.

So, remember earlier on when I told you about my low-budget, low-quality documentary? Well, here's a little bit more info about how that went down and why. When I moved back to Canada from Japan, I came back with a lot of questions about how young people make decisions about the future without knowing what they want or what's available to them. This led me to do a little bit of a study on my own.

To get a better understanding of how we're taught to make decisions, I decided to hit the halls of a couple of different schools to talk to the students and ask them about their decision-making process.

Armed with a very low-quality camera (it wasn't even digital!) and a sheet of questions, I began interviewing students in the halls of their colleges.

My goal was to get students talking about how they made decisions about which school to go to, which program to study, and if they were working, how they would choose their jobs or careers. By the time I was done, I had interviewed and spoken with almost one thousand students.

As I was shooting the video, I was shocked by the number of students who told me they simply opened the course calendar of their local college and chose something that sounded good.

I had so many questions.

Why weren't people choosing the stuff they wanted? Did they not *know* what they wanted? Why not? Is it possible for young people to know what they want and how to get it?

WHY WEREN'T PEOPLE CHOOSING THE STUFF THEY WANTED? DID THEY NOT *KNOW* WHAT THEY WANTED? WHY NOT? IS IT POSSIBLE FOR YOUNG PEOPLE TO KNOW WHAT THEY WANT AND HOW TO GET IT?

There were also hundreds of students who told me that their parents chose for them. I wasn't surprised at all when I asked the students, "Do you feel you made the right decision?" and they answered "no" or "maybe" or "I hope so."

Many of them told me they wished they could go back and change their decision or at least learn more about their options. So many of the people I interviewed told me they would have taken time off before rushing into another school. A bunch of them told me they would have gone to a different school or applied for a different job. Some said they wouldn't have gone to school at all, and many others said they would have learned more about themselves before jumping into any decision.

So many of the people that I spoke with seemed stuck. Their general mentality was that because they had started something, they had to finish it. So many said they couldn't consider making changes because they had already *wasted* so much time in their current program or on their current path. They were acting as if there were no way to repair what had already been done. They were acting like their school and work decisions were giant face tattoos of ice-cream cones.

Continuing with something because you feel bad about dropping out, quitting, or stopping sounds very Bob-like if you ask me.

Very few decisions in your life are so permanent that you can't pivot or make changes as you go along. Even face tattoos are (painfully) removable.

Going to a college that you know nothing about for a program you aren't interested in is choosing the "point, smile, and hope" method. Just showing up and filling a seat every day at school is pointing, smiling, and hoping. Staying with a boyfriend who isn't treating you well, assuming he will change, is pointing, smiling, and hoping. Sitting on your sofa with a bag of Cheez-Its waiting for something to magically happen to help you get into shape is pointing, smiling, and hoping. Applying for a job you know nothing about and aren't prepared for is pointing, smiling, and hoping.

Are you doing this? Or when it comes time to making a decision, do you hand your menu to someone else and say, "I don't know what to do. You order for me." Or do you get up and leave and do nothing at all? Or—do you try to figure out what you really want to do and make the best decisions for you and your future?

Making decisions doesn't have to be a lengthy process involving long lists, Google-like algorithms, technical diagrams, and lab tests. It can be as simple as asking yourself, "Is what I'm about to do taking me closer to the stuff I want to have, the places I want to go, the things I want to do, or the person I want to be?"

If the answer is yes, then the next move should be pretty clear. If the answer is no, that's equally as great! You can move on knowing that you're not missing out on anything.

Pointing, smiling, and hoping will almost always lead to surprises (*shirako* anybody?), and it will also often lead to regrets and confusion.

If you ever find yourself in a situation where you're feeling bad about a decision you've made or a decision that was less than informed and isn't working for you, then pause everything for a minute.

Take a step back.

Take some time to look at the decisions that led you to the feelings you're having and the situation you're in.

If you need to, make a list or a mind map of the decisions you made that resulted in those feelings or talk it over with somebody that you trust. Ask others what they would've done differently or simply ask for their advice.

There isn't one simple way to feel better about a decision you made that didn't work out in your favor, but if you're conscious of it and asking honest questions, there's a lot of learning, growing, and better feelings on the way.

You have all the power to figure out what your options are *right now* to start repairing the situation. How can you pivot? How can you get back on track to the things that you really want to be doing with your time, energy, and emotions?

As you move forward and become more aware, you'll begin to get much better at making informed decisions and understanding your menu of options.

VERY FEW DECISIONS IN YOUR LIFE ARE SO PERMANENT THAT YOU CAN'T PIVOT OR MAKE CHANGES AS YOU GO ALONG. EVEN FACE TATTOOS ARE (PAINFULLY) REMOVABLE.

7

UNDERSTAND YOUR MENU

Once you know yourself, know what your options are "out there."

YOU HAVE SOME DECISIONS TO MAKE. SOME ARE BIG AND OTHERS ARE SMALL.
UNDERSTAND YOUR OPTIONS, DECIDE WHAT YOU WANT AND HOW TO MAKE IT WORK,
AND THEN MOVE FORWARD.

→ One of the first phrases I learned in Japanese was *"kore wa nan desu ka?"* which means "What is this?"

I remember sitting down for dinner with my friend and his wife while she taught me this phrase and explained how it's the most important thing I could know if I didn't want to order *shirako* ever again.

For the entire dinner, I pointed to random things on our table repeating, *"kore wa nan desu ka?"* over and over again. On the train home, I pointed to signs, posters, and people, repeating my new mantra: *"kore wa nan desu ka?"* On the walk home to our apartment, I kept saying, *"kore wa nan desu ka?"* I think she quickly regretted teaching me that phrase, because she was the one who had to answer the question every single time.

Even now with the amount of Japanese I can speak, there are still some things I don't understand, especially when it comes to reading kanji. To read and understand Japanese, you need to know more than 2,000 kanji characters. I know about 350.

Every time I'm in Japan, there will undoubtedly be something on the menu I won't know how to read, but I make sure to ask, *"kore wa nan desu ka?"* before ordering anything. Sure, I don't always understand the answer, but I'm one step closer to understanding the menu. I might have to ask some other questions, have the server act it out, or draw a diagram, hopefully not of fish sperm, before I know what it is.

I haven't had *shirako* or *basashi* since.

Over the next few years, you will have a bunch of important decisions to make, and sometimes just the thought of trying to figure it all out is enough to make you want to hide in a dark closet, rocking back and forth and singing Justin Bieber songs to yourself under a *Sesame Street* blanket.

But decisions don't have to be so scary. It's possible for you to understand your menu of choices.

Kore wa nan desu ka?

When I first decided I wanted to travel around North America speaking to teens, I wasn't sure how to start. I didn't know how to get hired, where to find schools or organizations that wanted youth speakers, how much to charge, or anything else about the industry of speaking to young people.

Before getting started, all I knew was that I really wanted to share my stories, experiences, and ideas with young people around the world. Instead of jumping in, pointing, smiling, and hoping my way through, I did some research. I searched around and found two guys who were youth speakers in the United States, guys who were known for being great at what they do and who were making a huge impact on the lives of millions of young people.

I emailed one of them, Josh Shipp, who, to my surprise, responded. He told me he would help answer some of the questions I had. He also told me that he and another speaker I had found during my search would be holding "Youth Speaker Boot Camp" in Dallas, Texas, for new speakers like myself.

→ To learn more about Josh's youth speaker wizardry, general words of encouragement, and the more-than-occasional references to goats, follow Josh on Twitter @JoshShipp.

A few months later, I flew to Dallas to meet Josh. He talked to me about how to get started, how to market myself, how much to charge, which organizations to contact, and a lot of other valuable insight. Armed with his advice, support, and information, I returned to Toronto and put his advice into action.

Within a year and a half, I was getting bookings from all across North America, and two years later, I was being booked for the same events as the other elite youth speakers in the United States and Canada. And now, I'm the most requested youth speaker in Canada.

If I hadn't reached out to other speakers, I may never have become a speaker, or maybe things wouldn't have happened as quickly as they did.

If I didn't try to understand the decision I was facing, who knows what I would be doing now?

So if you're trying to make a decision about something you aren't familiar with or are a bit nervous about, decide to understand your menu before placing your order.

Before deciding, ask, *"Kore wa nan desu ka?"* Do research. Find other people who have been where you are now. Ask them how they did it. Ask them what they would have done differently.

Are you thinking about designing T-shirts to sell online? Find people who have done something similar and ask them about their experience.

Do you want to write a blog about limited edition Nike Dunk sneakers? Search the Web and find people you respect who are doing something similar, then ask them how to get started.

Are you thinking about going to MIT for computer science? Track down people who are in their first or second year and find out what they like and don't like about it. Ask them if they could go back and change anything, what it would be and why.

Most people are willing to help. They are open to being contacted by people like you and will answer your questions. Reach out to them. If they are in your area, meet up with them, buy them a coffee, and pick their brain.

SO IF YOU'RE TRYING TO MAKE A DECISION ABOUT SOMETHING YOU AREN'T FAMILIAR WITH OR ARE A BIT NERVOUS ABOUT, DECIDE TO UNDERSTAND YOUR MENU BEFORE PLACING YOUR ORDER.

If you run into somebody who isn't cool with you contacting them, well, those people probably hate kittens, drink beet juice, and smell like moldy Havarti cheese. And you can tell them I said that.

Just keep contacting people until you find somebody who is willing to help you understand your decision a bit better.

Sometimes, like me in Japan, you won't understand the answer and might have to ask some follow-up questions or do some more research, but then you will be one step closer to understanding your menu of options.

We live in an age in which we can contact just about anybody. Twitter, Tumblr, Facebook, LinkedIn, blogs, YouTube, Vimeo, and many other websites have been built (and will be built) with the idea of people sharing information with complete strangers.

There are sites that exist where users can log on and ask any question they might have about *anything* and have people in their network or people they've never met answer and give them feedback, advice, and resources.

→   Crowdsourcing is a great place to start your informed decision making. Asking questions of people you trust on your favorite social networks is a perfect way to start weighing options, getting feedback, and making decisions.

Of course, you're still ultimately responsible for the actual decisions you're making. Crowdsourcing your informed decision making isn't about handing the responsibility of your decisions to family, friends, and strangers. It's about collecting advice, opinions, resources, and experiences to help you make the best decision for you.

Every week, I get emails from people wanting to get involved with speaking, and I'm now in the position to help them understand the menu of options they are looking at. I'm now able to give them information to get started and decide if it's something they want.

You won't always understand your menu, but chances are you know somebody who knows somebody who knows somebody who can help or offer some way to help you figure it out.

If you don't take the time to understand your menu before making important decisions, then there's a good possibility that you'll have some raw horse and fish sperm coming your way.

The point is, before you dive into making decisions you aren't comfortable with, figure out what you are looking at, what your options are, and what you really want. Explore a little. Understand the decisions you are trying to make and what they could mean. Talk to people, ask others what their experience has been, and do whatever you can to learn about your decisions before making them.

To get what you want—and more important, to avoid *shirako* and *basashi*—you need to understand your menu.

EXPLORE A LITTLE. UNDERSTAND THE DECISIONS YOU ARE TRYING TO MAKE AND WHAT THEY COULD MEAN. TALK TO PEOPLE, ASK OTHERS WHAT THEIR EXPERIENCE HAS BEEN, AND DO WHATEVER YOU CAN TO LEARN ABOUT YOUR DECISIONS BEFORE MAKING THEM.

8

SLICE, DICE, & CHOP

Cut off all alternative options.

BUT IF YOU CALL NOW, WITHIN THE NEXT TWENTY MINUTES, YOU'LL GET A LIMITED EDITION KITTEN POSTER ABSOLUTELY FREE!

So not only am I an incredible battle rapper and karaoke singer. I also know a bunch of pointless information. Like this: did you know the word *decide* comes from the Latin word *decidere*? And did you know that *decidere* literally means "to cut off"? No? I don't blame you. But it does. Really. Look it up in the dictionary.

I know it seems incredibly pointless, but it's not. Actually, it's basically *Make Your Own Lunch* in one word. It's the only thing you would ever need to know to do the things you want to do.

Decidere. Decide.

Make a decision and then do it. No exceptions.

When you truly make a decision, you cut off every other option until you have achieved whatever it is that you decided to do. If there is something you want to have, then decide to have it. If there is something you want to do, then decide to do it. If there is somewhere you want to go, then decide to go there. And if there is something you want to be, then decide to be it.

This is how every inventor, actor, athlete, musician, teacher, author, pilot, scientist, police officer, and person in general has been able to do the things they have done.

And I know that you may be thinking, *But Ryan, you had no idea that Japan is what you really wanted. You even said so yourself...How do you make those decisions?*

Great question.

When I talk about cutting off every other option, I'm talking about creating a vision for yourself and your life, about making decisions like "I'm going to be healthy," "I'm going to be happy," and "I'm going to embrace adventure."

Once you make those decisions, the other ones become easier.

By no means am I telling you that you need to stress about how much milk you're going to add to your Corn Pops in the morning or which type of deodorant you're going to use before going to the mall later. I'm talking about making decisions about the bigger things. The things that you *decide* matter to you.

I decided that I would have adventure in my life at an early age, so when the possibility of going to Japan came up, I jumped on it. Once you've made a few of those bigger decisions, the other stuff becomes a bit easier. Don't worry, we'll talk about this more later.

Here's an analogy that might help: your bigger-picture decisions point your ship in the direction you want to go, and then your actions and smaller decisions that follow are the wind that pushes you closer to those things. Make sense?

Decision, combined with relentless action, is truly a superpower that can guide you to the stuff that you want.

DECISION, COMBINED WITH RELENTLESS ACTION, IS TRULY A SUPERPOWER THAT CAN GUIDE YOU TO THE STUFF THAT YOU WANT.

Decision is the reason you can learn a new language. It's the way that you can travel to awesome places and have incredible experiences. Decision is your secret formula for finding a career that you are absolutely stoked about.

If you look throughout history, you will find that anyone who has lived an epic life has done so because of his or her decision to do something.

Michael Jordan didn't accidentally become the greatest basketball player in history. He decided to be his best, which, as it turns out, was good enough to be the greatest ever. It wasn't magic either. It was more than simply making a decision and kicking his feet up and watching a few more episodes of an MTV marathon.

He pointed his ship in the direction he wanted to go, to the Land of the Greatest Basketball Player in History, population: one person. And then he made all of his actions and decisions on the basis of that direction.

If Michael Jordan faced the decision of whether to stay out late with friends or go home at a decent time so he could be up early and practicing, which do you think he would have decided? In order to be the greatest, which he wanted to be, he'd have to make the decisions and take the actions that went along with that decision.

Something tells me Taylor Swift didn't go to sleep and wake up with the words to "Love Story" written in her magical book of songs. Nope. She worked at her music, was rejected by record labels, and then worked even harder. When she had to decide between going to the mall to window shop for shoes and stare at boys, something told me she decided to work on her craft.

Jay-Z didn't unintentionally start a record label and mysteriously release hundreds of hit songs. He decided to be one of the bestselling artists in history, worked his butt off to get there, and has gone on to do so. If you listen to his music, he talks about his decision and hustle (a.k.a. action) to be the best.

Oprah Winfrey didn't stumble into success—her own television network, magazine, and media empire. She decided to do the things she's done and then took action to make them happen.

Bill Gates didn't wake up one day with a neatly wrapped package from UPS containing his fortune, innovations, success, and his awesome glasses.

Also, everything that has been invented, and will be invented, is the result of a decision or series of decisions and, equally as important, the actions that follow.

The airplane is the result of decision and relentless action.

The computer I am using to write this book is the result of decision and nonstop action.

This book is the result of decision and action.

Every book written before and after this one is the result of decision and action.

EVERYTHING THAT HAS BEEN INVENTED, AND WILL BE INVENTED, IS THE RESULT OF A DECISION OR SERIES OF DECISIONS AND, EQUALLY AS IMPORTANT, THE ACTIONS THAT FOLLOW.

You, as you sit there right now, are a result of your decisions and the actions you've taken. If you're tired, maybe you decided to stay up late (decision) watching music videos online last night (action). If you're feeling great, maybe you decided to go for a run after you finished school or work. If you're feeling down, maybe you're deciding to let something make you feel that way or maybe you're deciding to keep it bottled up and not get help.

It's hard to hear sometimes, but you are your decisions. You make your own lunch. Are you being Bob? Or have you decided to get the stuff you love? Do you *try* to do things, or do you *decide* to do them? There's a huge difference. Do you cut off every other option until you have the things you have decided to have?

Do you want to start making your own lunch? Then slice, dice, and chop: make real decisions and cut off every other option until you have what you want.

Want to land that job as a web designer? Then get laser-focused on your craft. Spend every free moment learning about design — pick up a class or take a certification program, hang out with designers and ask them to give you firsthand experience, talk about design and volunteer your services everywhere and anywhere you can to gain experience and build your portfolio. Aside from eating, sleeping, and family responsibilities, cut off everything that isn't bringing you closer to what you want to be doing and how you want your life to be.

Is that four-hour Xbox marathon bringing you closer? Nope? Cut it (not literally—electrocution is no joke). Another episode of *Teen Mom*? Really? Is that really bringing you toward the things you want? No? Cut it.

The difference between rich and poor, excitement and boredom, and success and failure is decision. I can't type it enough times: decision is the only way anyone has accomplished anything, ever. So instead of sitting there waiting for luck, destiny, or fate to deliver a gift basket to your front door, filled with money, Cherry Coke, cheese wheels, your dream job, and a private jet, decide to get it yourself.

You have the most incredible superpower (other than Wolverine's retracting adamantium claws, of course) to do whatever you want. That superpower is decision.

You hold the power to decide to be happy. You can decide to be more confident. You get to decide what to do with your life, when to do it, and how to do it. You get to create the future you dream of, and you can decide to change it at any time. You get to decide who you will be and cut off every other option until you've become that person.

You get to make your own lunch.

YOU GET TO CREATE THE FUTURE YOU DREAM OF, AND YOU CAN DECIDE TO CHANGE IT AT ANY TIME. YOU GET TO DECIDE WHO YOU WILL BE AND CUT OFF EVERY OTHER OPTION UNTIL YOU'VE BECOME THAT PERSON. YOU GET TO MAKE YOUR OWN LUNCH.

9

WHAT GOES IN MUST COME OUT

You can make decisions, but you can't "decide" the consequences.

FIBER KEEPS YOU REGULAR, AND TOO MUCH SWEET STUFF COULD PUT YOU ON THE "D-TRAIN," SO TO SPEAK. YOU CAN EAT WHATEVER YOU WANT, BUT YOU CAN'T CONTROL HOW YOUR BODY WILL REACT.

→ I was in seventh grade, and it was a long weekend. My friends—Stu, Matt, and John—and I had decided that the weekend was going to be special. Why? Because we were going to celebrate a holiday we invented. Earlier in the week, we had decided that the best name for our holiday was *Fire Day*.

Let it sink in for a minute.

Fire Day.

Fire Day celebrations would include lighting firecrackers and throwing them at one another, searching for clams and blowing them open with firecrackers, and, finally, lighting matches, placing them in dog poop, and spraying them with hairspray.

Genius.

We celebrated Fire Day in a government-owned conservation area near Stu's house.

After a few hours of our festivities, we decided that our first ever Fire Day was a complete success. We packed up our gear and started to head home.

We got to the road, where we met a woman who was staring past us with a shocked look on her face.

What she said next made my heart stop.

"Hey, boys, do you know who started that fire out there?" She pointed to the conservation area.

We turned around to see what she was pointing at. That's when we saw it. A twenty-foot-by-twenty-foot section of the conservation area was completely engulfed in eight-foot-high flames!

Not. Cool.

We immediately threw our stuff beside the road and frantically ran toward the fire. Matt got there first and dove into the river. He began madly splashing the river water into the fire as fast as he could. John and I ran right into the fire and began stomping it out, and Stu grabbed an empty McDonald's cup with a hole in the bottom.

Thanks, Stu.

All of us were running around panicking. In my panic, I looked over at John next to me…who was on fire!

"John, you're on fire!" I shouted, pointing at his pants. Flames were devouring the denim.

Screaming like a little girl at a haunted house, he jumped into the river. As he climbed out of the water to continue stomping the fire out, I noticed that one of his pant legs had melted off. He was too preoccupied to notice. And I was too scared to tell him.

The next thing we knew, we were surrounded by firefighters who were holding shovels and fire extinguishers. I was like, "Soooo…you guys can take it from here, right? We're going to go." The four of us ran to Matt's house to clean up and get John a new pair of jeans.

Epic fail.

So what does this have to do with *making your own lunch*? It doesn't get any simpler than this: there are two types of decisions—good ones and bad ones. That's it, that's all, nothing more, nothing less.

The things you decide all have a consequence or consequences. You can do everything in your power to make the best decision possible, but sometimes things just won't work out the way you planned. All you can do is make the best decisions you can for yourself and your future. Understand that bad things sometimes happen. And be prepared to stand by your decision or make the adjustments you need to.

Good Decisions and Bad Decisions and Really Bad Decisions

You're smart. How do I know? You're reading this book and you've set your Facebook privacy settings so that your dad doesn't see what you did to his car last weekend. You don't really need me to waste your time writing about what a good decision is.

So I will break it down the simplest way I can: a good decision is one that you make without having to worry about the consequence. Why? Because you're confident it was a good decision, no matter the outcome.

For example, you decide that you want a new job. You put together your résumé and fill out the application. Whether you get the job or not, it was a good decision to apply for the job. If you don't get it, it's OK. The world will not end, and you will be all right. And on the bright side, you applied for the job. You don't have to wonder what could have been, you know? And that's a good thing.

Bad decisions are a little different.

Fire Day was definitely a bad decision.

With bad decisions, you do one of two things. You blame or you avoid the consequences.

Blaming is pretty straightforward. It's when you try to blame someone or something else for the outcome of one of your decisions—like blaming the weather, nature, friends, alien abduction, parents, invisible friends, and imaginary pets for being late to a job interview.

As humans, it seems there is something embedded in our brains that says, "If something bad happens because of one of my decisions, it's not my fault." It's like we want to take credit only for the good stuff. But accountability is a huge part of making your own lunch.

I'm sure you can think of a few times you blamed somebody or something else for one of *your* bad decisions: your parents, your friends, your teachers, the weather, the bus driver, your dog, your horoscope, your church, your favorite sports team, a movie, a stranger, and a million other things.

The way to start living the way you want to is to realize that *you* are responsible for the good *and* the bad. This is called accountability. Consider when you stub your toe. Of course you didn't mean to. Why would you? Stubbing your toe hurts. Nonetheless, your decision to take that step resulted in a throbbing toe. We can control the choices we make but can't always control the outcomes. Accepting accountability for choices *and* their consequences is how learning happens. Oh, and you should probably watch where you're going.

Blaming is straightforward, but avoiding the consequences of a bad decision is something different. Avoiding the consequences of your bad decisions usually leads to more bad decisions.

When my friends and I were trying to sneak past the fire trucks after setting a forest fire, we were trying to avoid the aftermath of our terrible decision. In your case, not going home because you broke curfew is a double-decker avoidance technique. Lying about how the side of the car got dented is avoiding your bad decision.

THE WAY TO START LIVING THE WAY YOU WANT IS TO REALIZE *YOU* ARE RESPONSIBLE FOR THE GOOD *AND* THE BAD. THIS IS CALLED ACCOUNTABILITY.

You are bound to make bad decisions during your life. I have made hundreds, and I still make them. Just last month, I decided to grow a mustache. However, because I know the ideas and principles of *Make Your Own Lunch*, I know that when I make a bad decision, it's my fault, and I'm willing to accept that. I recognize how to make better decisions, decisions that will bring me closer to the things I want. I also know now that someone younger than fifty should never wear a mustache unless their last name is Norris and their dad's first name is Chuck.

Make the type of decisions you are proud of, not ones that you will want to blame on others. Not ones that you have to hide from people or make pacts to avoid, and not ones that involve mustaches, unless of course it's Movember.

→   Movember is an annual monthlong event in November that involves growing a mustache and raising money and awareness for men's health. Check out www .movember.com for more info.

Make the decisions that will bring you closer to the stuff you want to do, the things you want to have, the places you want to go, and the person you want to be.

It sucks sometimes to think that you made a bad decision, but avoiding it or blaming it on someone or something else is worse. Realizing that you were in control—and still are—is better than going through life thinking that you have no control.

In this life, you can decide anything you want, but you can never choose the consequences. Every decision you make will have a consequence, good or bad.

When you make a decision that has a good consequence, it's an awesome opportunity to look at what you did that brought you to that decision and that consequence. How can you learn from it? How can you use what you did the next time you are making a similar decision?

Got a killer score on your most recent test? Awesome. Why did that happen? Was it because you were really stoked about the course? Was it the result of a ton of studying? Was it because you did the reading? Or was it because you were looking over the shoulder of the smart kid in your class?

Next test, you know exactly what you need to do if you want a great grade. (P.S. Cheating is not cool…Wait, unless it's a video game, in which case, it's very cool.)

Likewise, when a decision brings a bad consequence, take some time to figure out why things didn't work out. Learn from the decision-making process that resulted in the consequence you didn't want. When you face a similar decision in the future, use what you've learned to avoid that consequence or outcome again. You can make the decisions you feel are best for you and your future and move forward with confidence.

You've made a ton of good decisions up to this point. Trust me. Sometimes you have realized it and other times, you may have just thought you were lucky.

Cheesy motivational moment: the sooner you realize that you are in control of your life, the sooner you can move forward. The sooner you make more awesome decisions, the sooner you can forget the terrible things that might have happened to you and the sooner you can rise above the crappy decisions you made in the past. The sooner you decide to take responsibility for your decisions, the sooner you can take action to start making things better and the sooner you can shave your mustache.

If you want things to change, realize that you, and only *you*, can decide to make changes.

10

GET HUNGRY

Begin making your ultimate list.

THERE'S A REASON FOOD COMPANIES ALWAYS SHOW YOU FOOD IN THEIR COMMERCIALS, BILLBOARDS, AND MAGAZINES. TO MAKE YOU HUNGRY.
THE HUNGRIER YOU ARE, THE MORE YOU'LL EAT.
IT'S TIME TO GET HUNGRY FOR THE STUFF YOU WANT.

I MADE MY OWN LUNCH

JORDAN

When he was in the fourth grade, Jordan Romero saw a mural in the hallway of his school that changed his life forever. The mural was of the seven highest summits in the world, summits that included Tanzania's Mount Kilimanjaro and the world's highest summit, Mount Everest.

When his dad picked him up from school that day, Jordan told him about the picture he saw and that it had inspired him to climb each one of those summits. This wasn't some random goal that he would maybe eventually start. He wanted to start right away.

So he did.

Between the ages of ten and twelve, Jordan conquered five of the world's seven highest summits located on five different continents. In May 2010, he completed his goal of climbing the world's seven highest summits when he stood at the top of Mount Everest.

→ To learn more about Jordan Romero, visit www.jordanromero.com.

How could a twelve-year-old kid do something that thousands of other people fail at doing?

Because he was hungry.

Jordan knew what he wanted, but he didn't stop there. He decided that it was absolutely realistic for him to accomplish his goal, and he started doing everything in his power to bring him closer to it. From doing climbing-specific physical training to imagining the climbs with his team, talking with local mountain guides, and mentally preparing for each climb, Jordan never let go of what he wanted.

He saw what he wanted and became so hungry for it that he cut off every other option until it was done.

So what does this mean for you?

This means that the hungrier you are, the more likely it is that you will want to eat. The more you see what you want to have, what you want to do, where you want to go, and the person you want to become, the more your mouth starts to water.

The more realistic it becomes, the more desperate you get to have those things and do that stuff.

The more you will start to take action.

Look at your menu. Start to get hungry.

Are you interested in traveling? Buy some travel magazines and start reading about other people's adventures. Head over to Flickr and browse pictures of the places you want to go. Check with your school to see if you have access to any travel programs or ask about exchange programs. Gather brochures, pamphlets, and information. Let your mouth water.

If you want to become a scuba-diving instructor, watch YouTube scuba-diving videos or follow some scuba-diving schools and instructors on Twitter. Connecting with other people on social media who are doing, or who want to do, what you want to do is such an awesome way to get hungry and feed off of each other's excitement.

So if you want to be a scuba instructor, start living the life of a scuba-diving instructor now. Hang out with other people who are interested in scuba diving, go to events and fund-raisers that they go to, and get involved with the movements and organizations that they are involved in.

→ Social media is the perfect way to get help with the things you want to do. Surround your virtual self with the people who are doing the things that you want to do and who are going where you want to go, contact them, and ask questions. People will help.

Start getting hungry for the things you want. Cut pictures out of magazines, bookmark websites, Photoshop your face on Brad Pitt's body (or Angelina's, or both), or create a collage or video with music that gets you stoked for the epic life you have decided you will live.

Start creating your personal menu. Just like a menu, include some appetizers or smaller things you want, like a picture of a fishing rod because you want to enjoy the outdoors more. And of course, include the main courses. Put some of the bigger things on there, like a picture of the Eiffel Tower to represent the trip to Paris you want to take. Or a cutout of the mascot of the college you want to attend.

Do whatever you need to do to get so incredibly hungry that you can't take it anymore. Imagine what it's like to climb that mountain, drive that car, take that trip, volunteer with that organization, go to that school, or do that job. Just get hungry!

Still not hungry enough? Let's try this. Dim the lights, light the incense, press play on your *Serenity Sounds of the Sahara* CD, and get ready:

What does your dream life look like?

What are you doing?

Where are you living?

Who are you with?

What do you have?

Where have you been?

Where are you going?

What kind of person are you?

What type of people are you surrounded by?

How does your dream life feel?

Seeing the things you want to have, the things you want to do, the places you want to go, and the person you want to become creates an appetite for those things. Your mouth starts to water, and you can imagine exactly what your life will be like.

I know that at first it may seem like you're just tricking yourself. It may seem like these things are far away, and you may never really get what you want.

You may be thinking, *Ryan, what's the point? My life sucks right now! I still live with my parents*, or *I'm only in high school*, or *I'm failing my courses*, or *I'm completely broke. What's the point of seeing my dreams? They are so far away.*

➔ A few years ago, I was speaking at a districtwide conference for high school seniors who were not going to college after finishing high school. Every student in the audience would be looking for work after high school.

After speaking for an hour, I stepped offstage and began chatting with some of the students. There was a moment in which I was surrounded by a group of students asking me questions. Questions about travel, questions about work, questions about my book, and questions about experiences. Off to the side, there was one young guy who was leaning against the wall, watching the group of students and me.

After the group of students slowly went off to their next workshops, the kid who was watching from the side approached me.

He looked up at me, and with his chin quivering, near to tears, he said, "Ryan, thanks so much for being here today and speaking to me."

Naturally, I said, "You're welcome."

He then said, "No. I don't think you understand. None of my family or friends knows that I'm here today."

I looked at him, confused.

He explained, "Do you have any idea how *embarrassing* it is when all of your friends are opening up their college acceptance letters, super excited about finishing school so that they can move on to something new and exciting, and you're sitting off in the corner like a complete *loser,* not having the slightest clue what you're doing after high school?"

We talked for a few minutes, and he told me how relieved he was to hear about some other options after high school. He even used the word *excited.*

Sometimes all it takes is knowing that there are options out there for you, options that other people maybe aren't talking to you about. Options you had no idea even existed.

It's OK to be a bit confused about what you're doing, and even scared, but don't let it have you feeling so overwhelmed that you don't do anything.

Start searching, start talking to people, start collecting experiences and information. Start getting hungry for something, for *anything*. Get hungry for your next step.

Now is not the time to be realistic. Now is the time to really start getting hungry.

Jordan Romero didn't stop to think whether his dream to climb the world's seven highest summits was realistic. He used a mural he saw when he was in fourth grade to get his stomach growling. He used that picture to get hungry. So what do you want to do?

Head to your local Thai restaurant and get hungry (literally) for the trip you want to take to Thailand.

Take an introductory course to scuba diving and get hungry for your scuba-diving license.

Rent a few French movies on Netflix and get hungry to learn French.

Volunteer for a few companies you think might be cool to work for to get hungry for an awesome part-time job.

Collect some college pamphlets and take a campus tour to get hungry about going to the college you've dreamed about for years.

Ask if you can shadow a welder in your hometown on the job for a day to get hungry about starting your welder apprenticeship.

Talk to your student council president about her experiences as the leader of the student body to get hungry about running for student council.

Join a salsa dance class at your local community center to get hungry about teaching salsa dancing.

Buy an obnoxiously large picture frame for the high school diploma you're earning to get hungry about graduating with honors.

Watch some online documentaries about Cambodia to get hungry about volunteering there.

Get hungry to start now.

Get hungry!

Now excuse me while I go make something to eat.

START SEARCHING, START TALKING TO PEOPLE, START COLLECTING EXPERIENCES AND INFORMATION. START GETTING HUNGRY FOR SOMETHING, FOR *ANYTHING*. GET HUNGRY FOR YOUR NEXT STEP.

Side Dish: Your Personal Menu

Twenty-One Questions to Get You Started

I'm not 50 Cent (in case you haven't figured that out by now), but I'll ask you twenty-one questions.

Think about the next three hours, the next three days, the next three months, and the next three years. Answer these questions to whet your appetite.

1. What three trips are you planning?
2. How are you making money?
3. How much money are you making?
4. Where is your next vacation?
5. Who are you with?
6. What kind of difference are you making in your school, family, friendships, community, and the world?
7. What's stopping you from doing what you want? Is it *really* stopping you, or are you making excuses?
8. What do you do on your weekends?
9. What do you do in your spare time?
10. What type of work do you do?
11. Are you furthering your education?
12. What are you known for?
13. If you could speak to the world about one thing, what would that be? Why?
14. What is one thing you've done in your life that you consider an accomplishment?
15. What is the best thing you get to do?
16. What do your friends turn to you for?
17. How are you preparing to have what you want, do what you want, go where you want, and be who you want?
18. Who do you turn to for advice?
19. How are you helping others?
20. How does helping others feel?
21. Are you really hungry?

STEP 3

YOUR BALANCED DIET: MAP IT OUT

11

THE FOUR FOOD GROUPS

Four decisions you can make right now.

EAT SOMETHING FROM EACH OF THE FOUR FOOD GROUPS EVERY DAY AND YOU'LL STAY RELATIVELY HEALTHY. MAKE DECISIONS FROM THE FOUR FOOD GROUPS OF *MAKE YOUR OWN LUNCH* EVERY DAY AND EPICNESS IS JUST AROUND THE CORNER.

So what do you want to be when you grow up?

That's easily the worst question ever. (Other than, "If I ate myself, would I become twice as big or disappear completely?" This is an actual question on Wikianswers.) If anybody ever asks you what you want to be when you grow up, you should kick them in the shins and splash lemon juice in their eyes. Or tell my mom and she will take care of it.

When you were a kid, do you remember how you would answer that question? In third grade, I remember going around the "sharing circle" (yes, we had a sharing circle—a circle where people shared stuff. I know. Clever, right?) and the students answered the question with answers like, "a fireman," "a police officer," "an astronaut," "a doctor," "a lawyer," and I remember thinking I didn't even know what half of those things were. I mean, I learned how to tie a lot of knots in Cub Scouts, but I had never heard of an "astro knot," and I had no idea how somebody could become one.

When it got to me, I blurted out the first thing that came to mind: "A rhinoceros!" It seemed like a viable career path for me at the time.

The class laughed.

The teacher frowned and wrote something in her teacher notebook.

In high school, it was the same thing. As a junior and senior, there was all this discussion about what everyone was going to do after high school. I heard things like, "I want to work with people, so I'm going to study psychology," or "I like working with numbers, so I'm taking accounting." When people asked me, I answered as honestly as I could: "I have no idea. A rhinoceros?"

The class laughed.

I frowned. The teacher wrote something in her teacher notebook.

I remember thinking, "How the heck am I supposed to decide what to do with the rest of my life while I'm in high school?" And I also remember thinking that everybody's answers seemed wrong for me. It was like they were reading a script somebody else wrote for them. And the script wasn't from an action or adventure movie. Why was there so much pressure to figure it all out right then, at that *very* moment? Do you need to have an answer by the time you finish high school?

My teachers, counselors, and friends were acting like I absolutely had to have an answer by the end of my senior year. And if I couldn't figure it out, I would end up shining people's shoes with strangers' spit for the rest of my life. They also acted like the world after high school was a brain-eating, zombie-infested horror movie in which everybody hated puppies and babies and drove old ice-cream trucks, offering children apples with razors in them. Yes, it was *that* scary.

After I graduated, I realized everyone was making things a lot scarier than they actually were. This wasn't the first time I experienced this.

➔ When I was thirteen, my home province of Ontario put a program into elementary schools where every student in seventh grade had to get a shot at school to prevent hepatitis B. I had no problem with this, even though the last time I had had a shot was when I was a baby, and I cried like, well, a baby.

Then the day came where my class was supposed to go to the gym to get our shots. "Have you seen the needle? It's thicker than this marker," one of my friends said as he held up a Magic Marker. (Why are they called Magic Markers, anyway?)

Another one of my buddies offered these comforting words: "Dude, it's going to hurt so bad. My brother had to get it and he cried for like sixteen hours." His brother was a tough guy with leg *and* armpit hair, and if it made *him* cry, what the heck would it do to me? I mean, I had a countable amount of leg hair and only a single hair in one

MY TEACHERS, COUNSELORS, AND FRIENDS WERE ACTING LIKE I ABSOLUTELY HAD TO HAVE AN ANSWER BY THE END OF MY SENIOR YEAR. AND IF I COULDN'T FIGURE IT OUT, I WOULD END UP SHINING PEOPLE'S SHOES WITH STRANGERS' SPIT FOR THE REST OF MY LIFE.

of my armpits. I was slowly starting to have a problem with this. Not the lack of body hair—the needle.

As the morning dragged along, things started to get worse. Kids in my class were talking about how much it was going to hurt. Half of the girls and one really sensitive guy started to cry. Some of my friends even called their parents and asked if they could go home. As we lined up to go to the gym for our vaccinations, some of my classmates were screaming, tears pouring out of their eyes, crying, "I don't wanna go!" or "Do I have to get it?" It was mayhem.

We got to the gym and things got worse. A lot worse. It was like a scene from a war movie. There were makeshift beds all over the place with kids lying in them, shaking and sucking their thumbs, all in a state of shock. Everywhere I looked, people were crying. A girl from our class fainted as we waited to get our needles. I remember thinking how lucky she was.

We sat against the wall and were called one by one to different tables where we were greeted by a nurse with a giant syringe she slammed into our arms until we screamed for mercy or passed out, or both.

"Ryan Porter, table sixteen."

This was it. It was time to say good-bye to my arm and masculine image. Because judging by all the screaming, I was going to cry…like an infant.

I sat down at the table. I couldn't bear to watch. I didn't want to see the monstrosity of a syringe that would soon be piercing my arm, leaving me scarred for life. I focused on the basketball net above my head, thinking sweet thoughts of basketball glory.

"You don't want to watch?" the nurse asked as she rubbed my arm with something cold.

"No thanks," I squeaked.

I bit my lip and prepared for excruciating pain. I began counting in my head. "Five…four…three—"

"OK, you're done," the nurse said, as I felt her rubbing my arm again.

I looked down and saw an X-Men Band-Aid.

"Wait. Done what?" I asked.

"I'm finished giving you the shot. You can go back to class."

"But I didn't…There's no…My arm is still…I didn't even feel it." I was confused.

"Because you're not supposed to feel it. Look how tiny the needle is," the nurse said as she proudly displayed a needle so tiny I had to squint to see the tip of it. But what about all the carnage? The bloodshed? The pain? Loss of life? Crying brothers? Why was I not lying in a bed, screaming for my mommy?

"But what about all of those people?" I asked as I pointed to the bodies strewn all over the place.

"Those are all the people who are too scared to get the shot."

People want you to believe that your life after high school is going to be so difficult, like you have to make one decision and have to get it right. They act like it's going to be painful if you can't get it figured out before you graduate. But, like I learned with my hepatitis B shot, it's not that bad.

PEOPLE WANT YOU TO BELIEVE THAT YOUR LIFE AFTER HIGH SCHOOL IS GOING TO BE SO DIFFICULT, LIKE YOU HAVE TO MAKE ONE DECISION AND HAVE TO GET IT RIGHT. THEY ACT LIKE IT'S GOING TO BE PAINFUL IF YOU CAN'T GET IT FIGURED OUT BEFORE YOU GRADUATE. BUT, LIKE I LEARNED WITH MY HEPATITIS B SHOT, IT'S NOT THAT BAD.

Instead of spending your time being afraid, anxious, nervous, or worried, you can relax a bit because you know it won't be as bad as people are making it out to be. You can spend your time getting excited about the things you will do and places you will go.

The truth is, you don't have to have all of the answers by the time you finish high school. In fact, you never need to know all of the answers. And here's a secret your parents and teachers probably don't want you to know. Most of *them* still don't have it figured out.

Don't get me wrong. I'm not saying that after high school, every day is going to be peaceful bliss with hummingbirds greeting you in the morning as you look out your kitchen window at dolphins playing in the ocean under rainbows made of Skittles.

And it's definitely not permission to spend forty-seven hours a day eating Fun Dip and playing *Angry Birds*. Why? Because, well, there aren't forty-seven hours in a day, and there are still decisions you need to make. "What do you want to be when you grow up?" isn't one of them.

I MADE MY OWN LUNCH

BRIAN

On the surface, Brian had it all figured out. As a high school student, he worked for the school's newspaper and declared journalism as his college major. He went off to the University of Iowa and then landed an internship at ESPN.com and later at the *Los Angeles Times*.

But if you asked Brian, he would tell you that he was basically on cruise control, doing what he "should" do, and he eventually entered his senior year of college completely confused.

For the first time in his life, Brian pressed pause and asked himself some questions:

- *What do I want?*
- *Why do I want it?*
- *How do I go about getting it?*

Those questions, combined with an awesome mentor, basically had a baking soda + vinegar impact on his life. (Don't know what I'm talking about? Stop reading right now, Google it, then go make your own volcano. You're welcome.)

Brian's questions led him on a yearlong trip around the globe. He and a friend then set out on a hitchhiking adventure across the United States on a quest to meet strangers and ask them about their stories. Brian *then* took some time to write a screenplay and work as a travel agent. He made documentaries about athletes and cancer survivors. He went back to school, met a girl (now his wife), and moved to South Korea.

After all of this, from the outside, Brian's life looked like a mess, but on the inside, he had never felt better or more connected to the things he loved.

His travel experiences and his outlook on life combined with his wife's passion motivated Brian to develop a new venture called On the Road Bus Adventures. On these excursions, he and his wife take travelers on the ultimate coast-to-coast road trip through the United States.

In Brian's own words, he's been on a bit of a "gap decade," creating and re-creating the person he is and the person he will be.

Brian is the perfect example of a person who never had it all figured out, who still doesn't, but who is constantly moving forward and making his own lunch.

"What do you want to be when you grow up?" is a terrible question to ask yourself because, newsflash, there isn't *one* answer, just as there isn't one question, either. There are four. I call them the Four Food Groups, because if you haven't noticed by now, I'm witty and cool like that.

Why the four food groups? Because just like eating things from each food group every day will help you be healthy and energetic, addressing these four decisions every day will allow you to stay hungry for the adventures you will have and to keep moving closer to the things you want.

The four food groups of *Make Your Own Lunch* are the following:

1. What will you have?
2. Where will you go?
3. What will you do?
4. Who will you be?

By answering these questions, you will create a bigger picture. Answering these questions allows you to live an epically epic life of epicness. Not just a job you will do until you retire, not just a course you will study in school, but a *life*—a life in which *you* call the shots and do what *you* want to do.

By making these four decisions every day, you will soon start to see how many

"WHAT DO YOU WANT TO BE WHEN YOU GROW UP?" IS A TERRIBLE QUESTION TO ASK YOURSELF BECAUSE, NEWSFLASH, THERE ISN'T *ONE* ANSWER.

possibilities are up to you. It's exciting! I love knowing I don't have to decide on just one thing. It's liberating knowing that I can come up with as many answers as I want and that I can change them any time.

You're also probably going to find that as you start to answer these questions, you are going to run into parents, teachers, friends, and Uncle Franks who get angry or jealous that you're thinking this way.

You may hear things like, "You can't do whatever you want all the time." Why not?

"You can't always get what you want!" Sounds like somebody got coal in their stocking this year or is listening to the Rolling Stones too much.

"You can't have your cake and eat it too." Umm, how else do you expect to eat cake?

"Yeah, but sooner or later, you'll have to decide on one thing." Says you.

"You will have to grow up eventually." Who said growing up meant forgetting who I am and settling for some watered-down version of what I really want?

Why can't you do what you want to do all of the time? Why would you want to waste your time doing stuff you don't want to do? (If it's not connected to something you want to do and you see no value in doing it, don't do it.)

So many people get stuck doing something they hate because they feel like it's a waste to stop. They feel like they've dedicated so much time, effort, and money to one path that giving up would be a waste of those things.

The exact opposite is true.

By staying on that path, a path they now know is not for them, they are wasting their time and effort.

If you are in this situation, stop right now. Stop doing that thing that you know isn't bringing you closer to the stuff you want to do.

I'll leave it at that for now, but we will spend a whole chapter on this in just a bit.

SO MANY PEOPLE GET STUCK DOING SOMETHING THEY HATE BECAUSE THEY FEEL LIKE IT'S A WASTE TO STOP. THEY FEEL LIKE THEY'VE DEDICATED SO MUCH TIME, EFFORT, AND MONEY TO ONE PATH THAT GIVING UP WOULD BE A WASTE OF THOSE THINGS.

Why do you have to decide on one thing? And since when did growing up mean forgetting about the amazing things you want to do, the awesome places you want to go, and the person you want to be?

These are things that people who hate what they are doing tell themselves to feel better about not doing what they want to do. Do you want to know how I know? Because the people who *are* doing the stuff that they want to be doing would never say stuff like, "You'll have to eventually choose just one thing," or "Make sure you have a plan B."

Will Smith silenced the plan B lovers pretty quickly when he said, "There's no reason to have a plan B because it distracts from plan A."

The people who *are* doing the things they want to do, going the places they want to go, will tell you things like, "You can do whatever you want," or "Dream big," or "Shoot for the stars," or "You can accomplish anything you put your mind to." Sure, all this advice is cheesier than old *Full House* reruns or Green Bay Packer fans, but they just don't know how else to tell you to stop listening to Debbie Downer McDownerson and start doing what you want.

The thing is, once you start creating the life you want to live, once you start making your list and checking things off, the feeling of empowerment and freedom becomes addictive. Once you see how powerful your decisions can be, how much control you really have, you will start testing how far you can push it. And why not?

Jay-Z started as a rapper, but once he realized how much control he could have over his career and that he could live the life he wanted to live, he started doing more things. He started a clothing line. He became a sports agent. He opened sports clubs all over the world, launched the careers of a bunch of different artists, made more albums, and, let's not forget, he put a ring on it.

It all sounds great, Ryan, really. Blah, blah, blah, make a decision. Blah, blah, blah, blah, live an epic life. Blah, blah, blah, marry Beyoncé. Where do I even start? What if I don't even know what I want?

Lucky for you, I'm going to answer that. Except the Beyoncé part.

So where do you start?

You start right where you are, right now, by reading the next few sections and making the decisions I ask you to make. Don't worry if you can't answer every question in detail. Start with what you know. Start with what you have. Start with where you are.

Just like any great adventure, you need to know where you are now before you know where you want to go next.

YOU START RIGHT WHERE YOU ARE, RIGHT NOW, BY READING THE NEXT FEW SECTIONS AND MAKING THE DECISIONS I ASK YOU TO MAKE. DON'T WORRY IF YOU CAN'T ANSWER EVERY QUESTION IN DETAIL. START WITH WHAT YOU KNOW. START WITH WHAT YOU HAVE. START WITH WHERE YOU ARE.

12

WHAT'S IN YOUR CUPBOARD?

Discover your skills and talents and how to make them work for you, and how to move forward if something's missing (without focusing on what's missing!).

YOU HAVE A TON OF TALENT. YOU HAVE A BUNCH OF THINGS YOU LOVE, STUFF YOU HATE, AND THINGS YOU WANT TO LEARN MORE ABOUT. IT'S TIME TO TAKE A QUICK INVENTORY OF WHAT YOU'RE WORKING WITH TO DECIDE WHAT YOU'LL DO WITH IT.

Before we really dig into the Four Food Groups, we need to figure something out…where are you?

Right now, I'm back in Japan, sitting on a bullet train somewhere outside of Hiroshima beside a snoring *sarariman* (a.k.a. salary man; a.k.a. office worker) whose head is slowly making its way to my shoulder and whose right leg has been violating my personal space for the past twenty minutes.

Where are you now?

This question is a bit deeper than your actual location, so you can stop looking around now.

I just really wanted to tell somebody that I am on a *bullet train* and the dude beside me doesn't seem as excited about this as I am.

Answering the question, "where are you now?" is about creating a snapshot of your life as it looks right now. It is not necessarily where you are physically. It is about you taking some time to create a map of what things look like for you. Kind of like those maps you find in shopping malls. You know the ones, right? A big red dot: "You are here." Those maps also have a legend and show all the shops, washrooms, restaurants, and exits.

An expedition is impossible to make unless you know where you're starting. Figuring out where you are now means taking time to think about you, the things you love doing, the things you hate doing, the things that get you stoked, and the things that put you to sleep. It means thinking about who you are friends with and who you want to be friends with.

Use the next few pages to create that map for yourself now. It will make sense eventually. For now, do my mom a favor and answer the questions in the following section the best you can, and if you need to, come back later and add to them.

Don't worry about right or wrong answers because this is *your* snapshot. (P.S. Feel free to write your answers right in this book.)

Without knowing where you are, you won't know how to get to where you're going. Ya dig? That's what these questions are for. They help you see where you are, what you have to offer, and where to go from here.

Have you ever been excited to start something but when it came time to actually start, you didn't do anything? It's probably because you skipped this part, the most important part: figuring out where you are now.

For example, you know you want to <u>help children living in poverty</u> and know you are great at <u>listening to people</u>. Why not use that skill of listening to other people to <u>volunteer at an after-school drop-in center for underprivileged kids in your community</u>?

The underlined sections can be replaced with your unique answers. Remember, you are making your own lunch. Your lunch has a recipe, and just as with any other recipe, you need to see which ingredients you have before you start making it. Your ingredients will help you figure out which recipe to use and what to make.

And just like cooking, you don't need to worry if you're missing something, because you can just add it to the list of stuff you need to make your own lunch. This is all about what's in your cupboard right now, at this very moment.

And just because you have the same ingredients as somebody else doesn't mean that you have to make what they're making.

AN EXPEDITION IS IMPOSSIBLE TO MAKE UNLESS YOU KNOW WHERE YOU'RE STARTING.

What are five things you love about yourself?

What are three things you would like to change about yourself?

What are you awesome at?

What do you suck at?

What would you like to learn more about?

What do you know a lot about?

What things do you do when you have free time?

What things do you do that make you lose track of time?

What three things make you really happy?

What do you do to unwind?

What are three things that frustrate you?

What one or two things would you love to teach somebody about?

Same Ingredients, Different Recipes

Just because you come from the same neighborhood, school, family, or group of friends as other people doesn't mean you have to do what they're doing, like what they like, or go where they're going. You can do something completely unique to you.

➜ I looked into my backpack and started taking the contents out one by one: one old woman's gray-haired wig, my dad's safety goggles from the 1970s, my friend's McDonald's uniform, and some black wax.

I was in the boy's bathroom of my high school, getting ready to surprise everybody with an incredible disguise for my twelfth-grade graduation photos. After checking the mirror one final time to make sure I really did look ridiculous, I smiled and almost forgot I had blacked out my front tooth with the wax. I laughed to myself, straightened out my wig, and stepped out of the washroom into the hallway. As I entered the cafeteria, one of my friends noticed me from a distance and burst out laughing.

All the graduating students were in the cafeteria waiting to get their pictures taken, and it wasn't long before the majority of them were staring and laughing hysterically. I did my best to remain calm and seem like everything was completely normal.

"Porter. Office. Now!"

Great.

I didn't even make it to the waiting area. A principal had seen me and ordered me to the office. Wig in hand, defeated, I lowered my head and walked to the office. My principal burst into the office waiting room.

"Ryan, what do you think you are trying to pull?"

I looked up at her from the bench I was sitting on. She was fuming mad.

JUST BECAUSE YOU
COME FROM THE SAME
NEIGHBORHOOD, SCHOOL,
FAMILY, OR GROUP OF
FRIENDS AS OTHER PEOPLE
DOESN'T MEAN YOU HAVE TO
DO WHAT THEY'RE DOING,
LIKE WHAT THEY LIKE, OR
GO WHERE THEY'RE GOING.
YOU CAN DO SOMETHING
COMPLETELY UNIQUE TO YOU.

"Take those stupid glasses off!"

I took them off and looked up at her again. "Miss, I was just trying to have fun, and I—"

"You are not allowed to have fun in my school! And where the heck did your tooth go?"

I had forgotten to wipe the wax off. #regrets

I don't know why this happened, but I couldn't stop myself from bursting out laughing. I don't know if it was the thought of what I looked like or the ridiculousness of her statement, but I couldn't stop laughing.

My principal apparently didn't like this because she finished our little pep talk with these words: "Do you know what I think is fun? Pictures. And guess what? You will not be in any of the pictures in this year's yearbook."

She gave me three detentions and walked out of the office, and just like that, I did not exist in my senior year of high school. Not a single picture on a single page of the yearbook. I was even banned from the picture of all the students in my graduating class that they hang in the hallway.

Here's the deal—everyone in your school or grade or family or class is taught the same things, but everybody interprets those things differently. When our teachers announced that photos for the graduating class of 2000 would take place in two weeks, some people heard, "Make sure you buy new suspenders and argyle socks for the photos," and others heard, "Time to grow a mustache." I heard, "This is your chance to try out the new wax for your teeth."

Everyone was meeting to take pictures for the same reason. I just decided to go about it in a different way. This decision was, according to my principal, stupid and worthy of punishment.

Regardless of what people like my principal think, you don't have to be like everybody else. You aren't doomed to the same life as family members or friends, because you get to decide how you will take the lessons you have learned, the skills you have acquired, and the talents you were born with to carve out your own path.

It's a lot like the *Iron Chef*. Two chefs show up on TV to battle it out for the title of Iron Chef. At the beginning of each show, an ingredient is announced. Competitors have one hour to put together a bunch of dishes using the secret ingredient. By the end of the competition, both chefs have come up with completely different recipes.

Same ingredients, different recipes—different results.

You don't have to be like other people in your family, you don't have to do the same things as your friends, you don't have to like the same bands as your girlfriend, and you don't have to follow the same path as everyone else in your math class.

You get to choose how you will use the same situations, talents, and opportunities that others might have to do what most other people don't.

As I learned from wearing my disguise for graduation pictures in high school, sometimes the things we decide upset the people around us. But as long as the decisions we make aren't meant to hurt anybody, you will be OK.

Two years after starting my speaking career, I spoke at a school where my old principal was working. She was very surprised to see me and hear of my success. And best of all, we were able to laugh about the graduation photo incident. (She never did apologize.)

I don't care where you are from, what color your skin is, what you believe in, how long your hair is, or what your last name happens to be. You might share some of the same ingredients as other people, but you get to create your own recipe with those ingredients. A recipe completely unique to you and the things you want. And just like in *Iron Chef*, sometimes people won't like the recipe you've created or the things you are doing, but if you are OK with it, that's all that matters.

Now, what do you do if you get halfway through a recipe and realize that you're missing some of the ingredients?

I'm glad you asked.

Missing Ingredients

Have you ever seen a really great chef at work?

The best chefs come up with their own recipes. If they get halfway through and realize they're missing ingredients, they make it work or get the ingredients they need.

YOU DON'T HAVE TO BE LIKE OTHER PEOPLE IN YOUR FAMILY, YOU DON'T HAVE TO DO THE SAME THINGS AS YOUR FRIENDS, YOU DON'T HAVE TO LIKE THE SAME BANDS AS YOUR GIRLFRIEND, AND YOU DON'T HAVE TO FOLLOW THE SAME PATH AS EVERYONE ELSE IN YOUR MATH CLASS.

I MADE MY OWN LUNCH

NICK

In 2007, my college classmate and good friend Nick was living in Dubai, the city he grew up in, and cashing in on the real estate boom.

Developers from all over the world were flocking to Dubai to buy property and build seven-star hotels, indoor ski parks, giant towers, underwater hotels, and islands shaped like palm trees.

Nick was never interested in real estate, but he went back home under the pressure of friends and family to do something with his business degree from college.

His real passion was film. Every weekend and day off, he volunteered his time to help produce music videos, commercials, web videos, and anything else he could get his hands on.

Then the recession hit.

The real estate market that was providing Nick with money to live and volunteer with film came to a screeching halt, and all of a sudden, Nick was forced to make a decision.

Nick decided to follow his passion for film.

His friends and family were completely against the idea. He had *zero* education or training in film and only a few bottom-level contacts, and he was quickly running out of money.

Nick made a decision: Bollywood.

After spending three weeks in Goa, India, making a plan, Nick decided he would drop everything to follow his passion and start working in film. He used the few contacts he had and his excitement for film to get a few odd jobs and meet people in the industry. Those odd jobs and hard work eventually landed Nick a job with one of the top-five Bollywood production companies.

When I asked Nick how he dealt with the fact that he had no experience or schooling in film, he told me how he made it work: "I worked harder. I volunteered more time. I sacrificed parties for work. I surrounded myself with people who could help, and I never stopped asking questions."

After spending some time learning all he could and meeting as many new people as possible, Nick made one more move. He went back to Toronto, but this time he went with a plan: a recipe.

He knew what he wanted, he knew the skills and experience he had, and he also knew what he was missing and that Toronto was where he would find it. Nick used his Bollywood connections to land a job in Toronto assisting in the production of music videos.

Nick now works with artists like Choclair, Saukrates, Fefe Dobson, Delhi 2 Dublin, the Trews, Low Level Flight, Down with Webster, Glenn Lewis, and more, making incredible music videos and learning as much as he can.

But he's not done.

Nick is going back to school to get a few missing ingredients, a few of the skills he's missing, to do what he really wants to do in the film industry and get his degree in film.

There may come a time where you start working through your plan and realize that you are missing some ingredients. You might be missing some experience, or maybe you don't have enough money, or maybe you need more education or training, or maybe you don't know the right people.

But just as if you were following a recipe while cooking, if you are missing an ingredient, you either make it work without it or go and get the things you need. Maybe you ask a neighbor for help, maybe you run to the store to grab it, or maybe you substitute it with something else. The thing is, you still make it work.

The same goes for the stuff that you want. I can guarantee you that there will be times when you won't have all the ingredients. You can make it work without them or go get those ingredients.

And just to be very, very clear: I am not suggesting you have a plan B, I'm talking about creating a path B. Your end goal doesn't need to change, but sometimes on the path to that goal, you hit a roadblock or something you're missing. This is when you take a step back, look at what you have, what you know, and who you know, and make a path B. You either move forward with what you have or make a detour to get what you're missing. But you never stop moving toward what you want.

You might be working toward your scuba-diving trip to Costa Rica but realize that your Spanish is limited to "Where's the bathroom?" and "She's not my sister." You can decide to learn some Spanish, travel with a friend who knows Spanish, or make the trip work without it.

You might want to be a photographer but don't have the money for school. You can decide to get a job to help pay for it, or maybe just start shooting and learning as much as you can online from other photographers and make it work without the schooling. Or maybe you find some other way to make it work.

The thing is, you will always find that you are missing some ingredients. You can never let that stop you.

If Nick let his lack of experience stop him from following his passion for film, he would still be in Dubai trying to sell islands shaped like palm trees or buildings that are actual Transformers. Instead, he is in Toronto working a job he loves, surrounded by awesome people, and doing what he wants to be doing.

If Jay-Z let his lack of a major record deal stop him from releasing his first album, we would never have known that he has "99 Problems." Instead, he started his own record label, released his first album on his own, and went on to make history. His end goal has never changed, but the path he took to it has.

If you let a few missing ingredients stop you from living your epic life, you will miss out on so many incredible experiences. Instead, move on without the ingredients, substitute them with something else, or find a way to get them.

I CAN GUARANTEE YOU THAT THERE WILL BE TIMES WHEN YOU WON'T HAVE ALL THE INGREDIENTS. YOU CAN MAKE IT WORK WITHOUT THEM OR GO GET THOSE INGREDIENTS.

13

FOOD GROUP I

Decide what you will have.

"So, Miss Nebraska, tell me, if you could have anything in the world, what would it be?"

"Well, I don't even need time to think about this
one. I would want world peace."

Puh-lease.

Yes, world peace would be the most amazing thing
ever, but you aren't fooling anybody with that blue-
sequined evening wear. Why don't you tell us what
you really want?

If Miss Nebraska was being honest with herself
and the rest of us, I'm sure her answer would've been
"a bacon double cheeseburger." This food group—this
decision—is all about the bacon double cheeseburger.

This decision sounds easy, and honestly, of the four
decisions, this one is typically the easiest to answer.
This is the time for you to start getting excited and
start seeing all the awesome things you will have and
how your life will be.

Don't feel bad for wanting *stuff*. Everybody wants
stuff. I want a ton of stuff.

Don't worry about trying to beat Miss Nebraska
on this one.

Don't answer "world peace" because that's what
you think you should answer.

Don't spend time worrying about *how* you will get
these things. Only worry about what you will have.

I MADE MY OWN LUNCH

KYLE

Meet Kyle MacDonald.

Kyle decided one day that he was sick of renting an apartment and that it was time to become the owner of a house. There was only one problem—he didn't have any money. This is when Kyle was struck with a flash of genius: he wouldn't have to buy a house because he could trade something for a house.

That was the next problem. He didn't really have anything to trade. He looked around his house and found the thing that he would trade—a red paper clip. There was nothing special about this paper clip. It was your regular, everyday paper-clipping paper clip. Kyle went online and posted a picture of his red paper clip along with this:

> This red paper clip is currently sitting on my desk next to my computer. I want to trade this paper clip with you for something bigger or better, maybe a pen, a spoon, or perhaps a boot. If you promise to make the trade, I will come and visit you, wherever you are, to trade. So, if you have something bigger or better than a red paper clip to trade, email me with the details at oneredpaperclip@gmail.com.
>
> Hope to trade with you soon.
>
> Kyle
>
> P.S. I'm going to make a continuous chain of "up trades" until I get a house. Or an island. Or a house on an island. You get the idea.

Shortly after posting the picture of his red paper clip, Kyle was contacted by two girls who wanted to trade him a fish pen for his paper clip. Done.

He then posted a picture of the fish pen with a similar note, asking people to trade something for the fish pen. Ten minutes later, Kyle had his second trade—a doorknob that looked like E.T.

That doorknob was traded for a Coleman stove, which was traded for a red generator. The red generator was quickly traded for an empty keg of beer, a neon Budweiser sign, and an IOU to fill the keg with beer. Kyle called this item an "instant party." Kyle put the instant party up on the Web and was emailed with a potential trade—the instant party for a snowmobile.

The owner of the snowmobile just happened to be a famous radio-show host in Quebec, Canada. Kyle accepted the offer and headed to Quebec to make the trade. Not only was it an awesome trade but Kyle had begun to generate some attention around this adventure. The snowmobile trade was covered by TV, radio, and newspapers. He was starting to build some hype around his paper-clip-trading idea.

The snowmobile and the press it received landed Kyle an interview on the Canadian talk show *The Hour with George Stroumboulopoulos*. During his interview, Kyle jokingly stated that the only trade he wouldn't make was for citizenry of a small town called Yahk in British Columbia, Canada.

The next morning, Kyle was woken by a phone call from a reporter who lived near the town of Yahk, British Columbia, offering to trade the snowmobile for a paid trip to Yahk.

Kyle accepted.

The trip to Yahk was traded for a cube van, which was eventually traded for a recording contract at a studio in Toronto. The recording contract was traded for a rent-free apartment in downtown Phoenix, Arizona, complete with return airfare from anywhere in North America.

That rent-free apartment was traded for an afternoon with rock legend Alice Cooper. That afternoon experience with rock-and-roll royalty was traded for a snow globe—a collector's-edition Kiss snow globe. The snow globe was unique and wanted by a movie producer who was willing to offer a speaking role in his next movie, along with room and board during filming, as well as return airfare from anywhere in the world.

Then something crazy happened.

Kyle was approached by the town of Kipling in Saskatchewan, Canada, to trade the role in the movie for a house on Kipling's Main Street, complete with a sculpture of the world's biggest paper clip on the front lawn.

Exactly one year from the day Kyle made his first trade, he moved into his new house. Insane in the membrane.

➔ For more info about Kyle, visit www.oneredpaperclip.com and read his book *One Red Paperclip*.

ADDED FLAVOR

Ready for an epic challenge? Play "Bigger or Better." Put Kyle's technique to the test. Find something around your house and start making some trades. Trade with family members, friends, or complete strangers. At our offices in Toronto, we have had some students do this challenge and get some remarkable things from trading. One student even ended up trading for a car!

The moral of the story isn't that anybody with a red paper clip and access to the Internet can become a national celebrity and eventually trade up for a house. The moral of the story is to decide to get what you want and cut off every other option until it's yours. Use what you have right now to start working toward what you will have.

The moral of the story is also, be creative! Yes, you will have obstacles and moments that stump you, but if there's one thing we learned from Kyle, it's to be creative when thinking about how to solve your problems. Be creative as you move forward and closer to those things you want.

Will it be easy? Nope. Will you have to work harder than ever before, sacrifice time, and use some creative thinking? You bet. Is it worth it? I think so. The point is this: there's a way to get what you want. Instead of focusing on all of the reasons you can't have it, decide what you will have, with no exceptions, and decide what you're willing to do to get it. So:

What will you have?

What will you have today?

What will you have this week?

What will you have this month?

What will you have this year?

Side Dish: All You Can Eat

When What You Love and What You Do Meet

Your life isn't either one thing or another. It can be both things that you want, and more. It doesn't need to be the basketball team or student council, travel or a "real job." It can be all of those things.

My youngest brother, Dallin, and I checked into a hostel in a place called Semuc Champey in the middle of the Guatemalan jungle and immediately struck up a conversation with three awesome girls from Austin, Texas. After educating us on the importance of taking antimalarial pills while in the Guatemalan jungle (which, of course, we hadn't brought), the girls shared some of their travel stories and talked about some of the things they were passionate about and what they planned on doing after their journey finished.

One of the girls, Leila, talked about her passion for travel and told me about discovering her love of writing early on in her life. She wasn't sure how she would do it, but she planned on traveling and writing for a long time. I wondered how many people she told that to, and I wondered how they responded.

As happens when traveling, we had to say good-bye the next day. The girls left for their next destination, and Dallin and I headed out to explore water-filled caves by candlelight. We exchanged contact information, and I "friended" the girls on Facebook soon after I got home. Almost immediately, some interesting updates started appearing on my feed—from Bali, Thailand, Malaysia. Soon there were videos of sea lions in New Zealand, photos from whale-shark spotter planes in Australia and hang-gliding adventures, and tons of other amazing things popping up pretty regularly on my friend feed.

Sure enough, Leila was out there doing exactly what she wanted to be doing, on her terms, and having the time of her life while doing it.

Along with these epic adventures she was having, she was posting links to her published writing. Leila was living her dream. It turns out that she had left "real work" for what she called "a million unknowns." She moved to Australia without a plan, knowing only that she wanted to continue writing and having amazing experiences. And that's exactly what she did.

As she traveled and worked in Australia, Leila's writing work started to pick up. She was getting a ton of work, which allowed her the freedom for even more traveling. She went from Australia to Bali, then Thailand and on to Malaysia. She then headed to New Zealand, where she spent time cave rappelling, hang gliding, glacier hiking, and swinging through canyons on the highest swing in the world.

I emailed her before writing this section of the book to get permission to use a few of her experiences, and she sent her reply from Hawaii, where she was spending two months writing, exploring, and relaxing. You can follow Leila on Twitter (@leilakalmbach) and read stories about people she's met at www.howwelivestories.com. Have you ever heard the phrase, "You can't have your cake and eat it too?" Guess what, you can. It's the only way you'll get to eat cake.

Leila has her cake and eats it too…all the time. It's not always easy. In fact, she told me, "Living your dream doesn't always happen the way you dream it, but it's real and that's way more important."

You aren't like Bob, our peanut-butter-sandwich-eating friend at the beginning of the book. You are standing at an all-you-can-eat buffet at which you get to have exactly what you want. You don't have to choose between the sweet-and-sour pork and chicken balls. You can have both. Wrapped in bacon. Stuffed into a turkey. Deep fried. Covered in cheese and icing sugar.

You can stay away from things you don't want.

You can try new things.

You can go back for seconds and thirds, and best of all, you can have as much dessert as possible.

You are raised thinking you have to choose this or that. You *can't* have your cake and it too. You *can't* travel the world and work a real job. You *can't* design skateboards for children in third-world countries *and* be a successful businessperson.

Guess what?

You can. It's all-you-can-eat.

Leila has learned this through her travels and writing business.

Your world is a lot like a buffet—sometimes you can't fit

everything onto one plate. Sometimes you have to go back a few times to get everything you want. But often you can squeeze it onto the same plate.

Maybe now it's travel and later it's school. Maybe it's school while traveling. Maybe it's volunteering at an animal shelter now and studying to be a graphic designer later. Or maybe it's doing graphic design for an animal hospital while you volunteer there.

When I moved back from Japan, I thought I had one of two choices: (1) work in a field where I could use Japanese daily or (2) lose my drive to study and ability to communicate in Japanese and work a job that had nothing to do with Japanese at all.

Turns out I can run my business and still use Japanese daily. I rarely use Japanese for work, but I'm able to talk with friends on Skype, watch TV shows online, and meet people from Japan when I'm traveling.

The Internet makes the world a very, very small place. It used to be that if you want to study a new language or learn web programming or build a photography portfolio, you'd have to pay money and go to school to learn what you needed to get started. Now, you are always just a few clicks away from getting started, and many times, it's free or super cheap.

You can learn just about anything you want to learn by connecting with people, companies, schools, and tutors online. You never have to wait to get started learning, connecting, and moving forward. You have the power to do all that in your pocket on your smartphone, in the school computer lab, or at the library down the street.

When I first started in business, I didn't think I could be myself, dress the way I want, speak the way I normally do, and be respected as a successful entrepreneur. All the successful business people I knew when I was starting out wore pin-striped suits and always did up their top button on dress shirts.

I owned only one button-up shirt, and it was missing the top button.

I thought I would have to sacrifice a little bit of who I was to get what I wanted. Turns out I didn't. I have the freedom to talk and dress how I feel comfortable, and I've earned respect as an entrepreneur, speaker, and expert in my field.

So if somebody tells you that you can't have your cake and eat it too, throw a pie at him and eat the cake. You *can* have your cake and eat it too. You can find a way to do all of the things you love.

Sometimes, you'll be able to do them at the same time; other times, you might have to do them separately. But the best part of a buffet is going up and seeing what you missed the last time, trying new things, and stacking your plate sky-high full of the stuff you love.

14

FOOD GROUP II

Decide where you will go.

→ In the summer of 2004, I was in Nagasaki, Japan, as I had signed up for a weekend tour of some historical sites. My tour group members, all over the age of sixty and all Japanese, seemed very confused by my presence. I was neither old nor Japanese and spoke *maybe* five Japanese words at the time. Three of which were animal names.

First stop, the A-bomb Peace Park. A few minutes after we arrived, it appeared as if the tour guide was telling stories about the bombing. Everyone was serious. One woman was crying. This was when I finally understood my first word of the tour. As the tour guide pointed to the sky, she said in a spiteful voice, "America."

Every member of the tour responded with a slight gasp. Then, all at once, every single one of them turned around and looked at me. There I stood, wearing a Tupac T-shirt, baggy jeans, and Reebok sneakers. I don't know what an "American" is supposed to look like, but I definitely looked like one.

This is when I started doing something that we all do when speaking with people who might not understand our language. Our thought process is something like, "I know you don't understand my regular English, but maybe you will understand my sloooooow, *loud* English."

"Noooooooooooooooooo I aaaaaaammmmmm Canaaaaaaaaaaadiaaaaaaaaaan."

That night, in our traditional-style hotel, feeling bad about my Peace Park experience and preparing to join the tour group for dinner, I opened the closet in my room and made a discovery of heroic proportions: a men's kimono.

Perfect-plan formula: I'd put it on and go to dinner. When everybody saw me, they would forget about me being "American," and see how much I respect Japanese culture.

I was late for dinner because it took me, like, twenty minutes to figure out how to tie the belt of the kimono. I opened the door to the dining room and found a massive traditional Japanese room with tatami mat floors and no chairs. Everybody was kneeling at the small tables placed in rows throughout the room.

I felt hundreds of eyes following me to my seat in the middle of the room. I adjusted my kimono so I could kneel comfortably at the small table and began eating.

A few of the elderly people from my tour group looked at me and gave me approving bows. One of the cooler old guys gave me a thumbs-up. Mission accomplished. Or so I thought.

After about fifteen minutes of kneeling, the pain in my knees was unbearable. I felt my face turning red and the sweat forming on my forehead. I was completely uncomfortable. The woman beside me must have noticed because she called one of the waitresses over and began asking her something in Japanese. A minute later, the waitress came back with a small chair with no legs that she placed behind me. The older Japanese woman beside me motioned for me to stop kneeling, sit on the chair, and place my legs under the table. I looked around the room to see a few other people using these small legless chairs.

I was so relieved.

I slid my legs to the side of my body and started to stand up. This is when it happened. As I got to a half-standing position, I realized something. I had been kneeling for so long that I had cut off the circulation to my legs, and I had no control over what was happening.

Next thing I knew, I was lying flat out on the mats, the front of my legs soaked in soy sauce, and I was flopping around like a fish out of water trying to stand. My legs were so badly asleep that it took me about a minute to scramble to my feet, and as I did, I noticed for the third or fourth time of the trip, everybody was staring at me.

To make things right, I did what I saw Japanese people do to apologize. I started bowing. Frantically. Spinning in circles, bowing in every direction, saying, "I'm sorry. I'm so sorry. *Sumimasen*." As I made my final spin, I saw a mother covering her young daughter's eyes.

Confused and slightly offended by this, I bowed one more time, and directly in front of me on the ground, I saw the belt from my kimono. Looking down at my body, I saw that my kimono had come open, and everybody was staring at me standing there in my underwear.

The reason I'm sharing this story with you is not so you can laugh at my ridiculousness or to demonstrate how culturally sensitive I am. It's because this couldn't have happened anywhere else in the world, at any other time. Travel is one of the most amazing things we have the chance to do. It has a magical ability to teach you things that you wouldn't learn otherwise.

A volunteer placement in Spain can help you learn Spanish faster than you could imagine. A café conversation with locals in a small town in Germany could teach you about German history. Drinking tea with some college students in Tokyo could give you amazing insight into Japanese culture. Haggling a cheaper price on some souvenirs in Bangkok could teach you about negotiating or communication.

More important than learning about "stuff," travel has the awesome ability to teach you about *you*! You can learn what you're passionate about, you can learn what really makes you angry, what really makes you happy, what you really value, and who your real friends are.

Travel will scare you. Travel will intimidate you, and it will make you sick. But travel will also teach you patience, love, compassion, adventure, and understanding. It will open your mind to people, places, experiences, and ideas that you couldn't have gained doing anything else.

Travel has the ability to change you. The way you think, the way you view the world, the stuff you want, and the things you want to do.

You need to travel.

We live in a time where the world is completely accessible. You can travel just about anywhere in the world, without restriction. Sure, some countries, at certain times, are dangerous. But in my experience, the news, your parents, teachers, friends, and you are usually wrong about what is going on in other countries. Or maybe not wrong, just not fully aware of how great most places are.

The media tends to focus on the problem areas and bad news from different countries, and because the media is where many people get their information, the result is that misinformation circulates about people and places.

Travel doesn't mean you have to take five years off to backpack Europe, grow the world's longest beard, bathe in public fountains, and eat pigeon food.

TRAVEL WILL SCARE YOU. TRAVEL WILL INTIMIDATE YOU, AND IT WILL MAKE YOU SICK. BUT TRAVEL WILL ALSO TEACH YOU PATIENCE, LOVE, COMPASSION, ADVENTURE, AND UNDERSTANDING. IT WILL OPEN YOUR MIND TO PEOPLE, PLACES, EXPERIENCES, AND IDEAS THAT YOU COULDN'T HAVE GAINED DOING ANYTHING ELSE.

Travel can mean a weekend trip to a different city or a weeklong road trip to see your favorite team play in another state. It could be spending a few days at your aunt's cottage or camping in the Rockies.

Travel could be volunteering to collect data from monkeys in Costa Rica or nursing sick elephants in Thailand. It could be kendo classes in Japan or working at an English school in Uruguay. The point is that travel is necessary.

This is usually where people either start to get really excited or slightly angry.

But Ryan, travel is so expensive! How am I supposed to afford it? I can't just leave everything and go somewhere!

That's a lie. It's a lie that people who are afraid to push themselves out of their comfort zones tell you! Travel is not expensive. Staying at five-star resorts and drinking the finest wines from gold-plated goblets while getting a hot stone massage is expensive.

You can work any part-time job, for minimum wage, for a few months, and save enough money to buy a plane ticket to just about anywhere in the world. Anywhere. And once you get there, you can stay in youth hostels, or with friends or relatives, or you could couch-surf by using Couchsurfing.org to find who is in the area offering free, safe accommodation. Or you could find part-time legal work, depending on which country you go to and whether you have a visa that permits you to work.

HOW TO TRAVEL LIKE A PRO

1. Select a destination

Many destinations have seasonal prices. For example (in my experience), flights to Japan are more expensive in the summer than in the fall. For the best deals, choose a destination that is off peak season. Use websites like Hipmunk.com and Mobissimo.com to compare flight prices.

2. Calculate trip cost

Once you have a destination, start calculating the cost of everything. Start by choosing accommodation. Use sites like Couchsurfing.org and Hostels.com to find reviewed, cheap, and sometimes free accommodation. Use sites like TripAdvisor.com and Google to estimate the price of food and attractions. Check WorldNomads.com and other well-known travel insurance sites to get the cost of traveler's insurance.

3. Save money

Now that you know approximately how much the trip is going to cost, you know how much money you need to save. Of course, the quicker you can save money, the quicker you can go on your trip, so you might want to start saving as much as possible.

4. Investigate your destination's entry requirements

Every country has different entry requirements. If you're an American going to Canada, a passport is fine. If you're a Canadian going to the United States, you'll need a passport and you'll need to pretend that our national hockey team isn't better than the U.S. team. Some countries require you to apply for a tourist visa in advance of arriving; for others, you can do so on the spot when you arrive. Google is your friend. A simple search will give you the entry requirements for various countries.

5. Have an epic adventure

An epic adventure starts with an open mind. It starts by meeting new people, doing (safe and smart) things that you wouldn't normally do at home, like waking up early and heading to the local fish market or volunteering on a farm.

Twenty years from now, you will be more disappointed by the things you didn't do than by the ones you did do. So throw off the bowlines, sail away from the safe harbor. Catch the trade winds in your sails. Explore. Dream. Discover.
—Mark Twain

I spend less money on the road than I do when I'm home. In Guatemala, my hostel cost less money per night than a chocolate-banana smoothie from Starbucks.

Even in Japan, which is always considered one of the most expensive places to visit, I pay on average twenty dollars a night at youth hostels. I find restaurants where everything on the menu is 280 yen (approximately $2.80) or eat from vending machines or convenience stores, and it's all delicious and relatively healthy.

Traveling doesn't need to cost tens of thousands of dollars. It can be affordable. And to tell you the truth, the trips where I had to get creative about stretching my money always ended up being the best ones.

THREE TIPS FOR STRETCHING YOUR MONEY WHILE TRAVELING

1. Eat cheap

One of the best ways to save cash while traveling is by avoiding the expensive restaurants where all the tourists go to eat. Find the cheap local food by asking around or just watching where the local people are eating. You may have to leave the main tourist streets or buy your meal from a street vendor, but you'll definitely save some money.

2. Sleep cheap

Five-star hotels are awesome. They're also expensive. Save money on accommodations by staying in youth hostels. There are many websites to help you find the cleanest, safest ones, and as a bonus, hostels are an awesome way to make new friends. Check Hostels.com, AirBnB.com, and Couchsurfing.org to get started.

3. Go cheap

In many countries, taking a taxi is expensive. Save money by taking local buses or by riding the subway—or if you're really adventurous, rent a bike. The point is, stay away from private transportation, and you'll have more money left over to buy souvenir magnets for all of your friends and family.

So where will you go? What places are on your list? Where will you go this weekend? Where will you go this summer? Where will you go when you finish school?

15

FOOD GROUP III

Decide what you will do.

Most people assume that Food Group III is about the question, "What do you want to be when you grow up?" But you are smarter than most people, and so you know it's more than that.

On a flight from Chicago to Kansas City, I sat beside a middle-aged guy who I later found out was a carpet salesman. As the plane was taxiing down the runway for takeoff, he turned to me and asked the most dreadful words: "So, what do you do?"

Usually, when people ask me that question, I hit them with an "I'm a disposable camera repairman." That's when they look like someone just told them that the tooth fairy is really a seven-foot hairy dude with six arms and no teeth. But this time, I decided to answer it differently: "Well, sometimes I snowboard. Other times I speak all over North America to high school students. I spend a lot of my time working on RaiseYourFlag .com with my cofounder. Lots of the time, I sleep. I run. I work out. I travel. I sing (I'm terrible, but I still do it). I shower (yes, shocking). I eat. I burp. I fart (sorry, Mom—it's a natural bodily function). I study Japanese. I read a lot. I walk my dog. I listen to music. I sketch. I canoe. I camp. I hike. I floss. I surf the Web. I recycle. I do my own laundry. I run a successful business. I take pictures and make videos."

I then turned to him and asked, "So, what do *you* do?" He pulled out the *SkyMall* magazine from the seatback in front of him and began pretending to shop for foot massagers.

Often people define their lives by the job they have

or the program they're enrolled in at school, and it's usually the most boring thing about people. Don't limit yourself to doing that. You are so much more interesting.

When your parents were kids, the question, "What do you do?" probably made sense. I mean, people used to go to high school, go to college, get a job, and work that job until they retired, but now things are different. Statistics say that it will be rare for you to work one job for the rest of your life.

Most people define their lives by their job. I *am* a teacher. I *am* an electrician. I *am* a car salesperson. I *am* a doctor. I *am* a stay-at-home dad. I *am* a graphic designer. Even college students take this approach: I *am* an engineering student. I *am* an art major. I *am* a student at Greatest State University (pssst, that's not a *real* college). If you think your job is all you are going to do, you are completely wrong.

Decide the things you want to do. This could mean what you want to do with your life, or it could mean what you want to do during your summer holidays. It could mean the jobs you want to have or the actions you want to take. It could be anything from learning a new language to volunteering at your local food bank or starting a charity for children living in poverty in a third-world country.

What things do you want to do that will create the most fun, excitement, and fulfillment in your life?

Do you want to speak another language? Do you want to go skydiving? Do you want to learn how to tango? Do you want to travel to outer space? What are the things you want to do?

Next time somebody asks you, "What do you do?" tell them!

But Ryan, how do I know what to do? How do I start figuring it out?

You start by trying new things and having new experiences. You start by going to new restaurants and talking to new people. You start by making new friends, listening to new music, and doing things a little differently than you normally do.

Maybe for you, getting started means talking with your parents and asking them about what you loved doing when you were a kid and seeing if it's something you're still interested in or something you want to reconnect with. Maybe you start by making lists of things you want to try.

You can start by signing up for clubs and groups at school you might be interested in. You can start by volunteering your time to work on things you're passionate about. You can start by getting off the sofa and doing things. It's these small changes and these experiences that can transform the way you look at your future and the things you want to do.

What do you love doing? And when you're doing it, do you lose all track of time? What do you want to be good at? What are you interested in? This is a

MOST PEOPLE DEFINE THEIR LIVES BY THEIR JOB. I *AM* A TEACHER. I *AM* AN ELECTRICIAN. I *AM* A CAR SALESPERSON. I *AM* A DOCTOR. I *AM* A STAY-AT-HOME DAD. I *AM* A GRAPHIC DESIGNER. EVEN COLLEGE STUDENTS TAKE THIS APPROACH: I *AM* AN ENGINEERING STUDENT. I *AM* AN ART MAJOR. I *AM* A STUDENT AT GREATEST STATE UNIVERSITY. IF YOU THINK YOUR JOB IS ALL YOU ARE GOING TO DO, YOU ARE COMPLETELY WRONG.

great place to start. What could you do that uses those things? What could you do tomorrow that allows you to feel the way you want to feel?

Warning: don't be lame with this. It doesn't mean what you want to do for work. What do you want to *do*? What would create excitement for you? What can you see yourself doing next week, one year from now, in three years?

Eventually, you have to choose just one thing, right? Wrong! This Food Group is all about taking time to figure out what you actually want to do with your time and energy and then taking the steps to do those things. It's not about choosing one single thing you'll do for the rest of your life.

Some mornings, I wake up and study Japanese. Most mornings, I go to the gym. Some days, I travel around speaking; other days, I'm in my office writing or answering hundreds of emails from students across the continent. Some days, I do nothing related to work and hang out with buddies to play Xbox or basketball. Other days, I meet with my creative teams to figure out the direction of our website or marketing material, and some days, I just lounge around and read for the entire day in my pajamas.

I'm not telling you this to brag or to make it seem like I have this picture-perfect life. Some days suck. A lot of days are hard. Some days, I fail miserably at getting things done. I experience rejection almost every day. Some days, there are things that I don't feel like doing, but because they are connected to the things I want to do, the places I want to go, the things I want to have, and person I want to be, I do them.

I MADE MY OWN LUNCH

PAUL

As he was growing up, Paul Munro's interests were always changing, but there was one thing he knew he loved—skateboarding.

Like most other skaters, he knew that eventually he would have to grow up and trade in the skate park for homework. When it was time to start looking for work, he tried his hand at what seemed to be a million different industries. He really liked a lot of his jobs, but for some reason he couldn't figure out, he knew something was missing.

In the middle of his "what the heck should I do with my life" mini-crisis, Paul hopped on a plane and headed for Indonesia. Because that's, of course, exactly what to do when you don't know what to do. He stayed at a local youth center that happened to have a skate park where they held skate sessions two or three times a week. Teens could come, skate safely, and meet people in their community who really wanted to help them.

Paul knew he was in the right place.

He joined a session one day and noticed that the equipment the kids were skating with was in terrible condition. He was scared to try anything on the boards because they were pretty much corn chips on wheels, ready to break at any moment. He approached the manager of the youth center and asked about the equipment and where it came from. The manager told him that all the skate gear was donated from backpackers and people passing through.

Without even thinking about the hows or whys, Paul promised the manager that as soon as he returned to his home in Australia, he would send ten brand-new decks to the youth center for the kids to use.

On the plane home, it hit him. Paul wanted to get skateboards into the hands and under the feet of kids around the world who might not have the chance or money to buy their own new skateboards. He also decided that this project could be a lot cooler if he involved designers from around the world to help with the skateboard designs.

Boom! The Three Sixty Project was born.

Paul came up with a plan that every design they chose would become a limited-edition deck. And for every deck they sold through his website (www .threesixtyproject.com), they would donate one skateboard to kids in poorer countries who wouldn't otherwise be able to buy a new deck.

Within the first few months, Paul had donated skateboards all over Australia, Indonesia, Cambodia, and the Philippines. The Three Sixty Project is now growing and getting prepared to send decks to Uganda, South Africa, and many more countries.

Paul is a living legend who decided that to make his own lunch, he would have to be involved with something he was passionate about. Now, as he travels the globe handing out skateboards to kids in need and running a successful nonprofit, he knows he's in control and doing something he is infinitely passionate about.

→ Follow Paul and the Three Sixty Project @threesixtyprjct.

Your epic life starts when you realize that you can do exactly what you want to do for work, with friends, with your family, in school, tomorrow, this weekend, and every other day that follows. That's how you make your own lunch.

If you can connect with those things you really love and refuse to settle for anything else, you will never feel like you're working. You won't spend your workweek or school week counting down the hours until Friday and hitting the snooze button 629 times on Monday mornings.

The coolest thing about this is that you can literally try whatever you want with nothing to lose. With the amount of information you have at your fingertips, you can find almost everything you need to know to try anything.

Do you want to start a website selling Pokémon cards? Great, you can do that. You can find out how to start it, how to set it up, how to market it, and how it could be successful.

You want to make custom bicycles? Awesome. You can find somebody locally who is already doing it and ask them to guide you. They might even let you come in and job shadow or be an intern.

Are you interested in speaking Mandarin? There are resources on the Internet that can get you started. Stuff like videos, books, tutorials, podcasts, lessons, blogs, free software, and other people you can contact who are also learning Mandarin are just a few Google searches away.

The Internet puts you on the same playing field as almost everybody else. Use it, get the info you need, and then start doing exactly what you want.

What are you waiting for?

This brings us to an important part of this decision: the aftertaste.

Aftertaste

You should know something.

You have the power to change your family, your school, your friends, and your community forever.

How will you use that power? How will you leave your legacy?

As much as this "decide what you'll do" food group is about you carving your life's path and connecting with things that you are stoked about, it's also about leaving your legacy.

It's about using some of your time to give back, to work toward something bigger than you, something that could change the world of one person. That's what legacy is about. Legacy isn't about changing *the* world; it's about changing *a* world.

I can't think of a better example of this than Terry Fox. For those who haven't heard his name before, let me give you an extremely brief synopsis of who this incredible modern-day hero was.

In 1977, an eighteen-year-old teenager named Terry Fox, born in Manitoba, Canada, was given the news that he had osteosarcoma, a form of cancer, in his right leg from the hip down. He was told that his leg would have to be amputated. Imagine for a minute how this type of news would change your life.

Three years after his surgery, Terry, who was always an athletic guy, decided to run from one coast of Canada to the other to raise money for cancer.

LEGACY ISN'T ABOUT CHANGING *THE* WORLD; IT'S ABOUT CHANGING *A* WORLD.

He wasn't running to cure cancer for the world. Instead, he was doing it because of the kids he met with the same disease. He wanted to make sure that, in the future, those kids wouldn't have to suffer through the same thing he did.

He started his run by dipping his leg in the Atlantic Ocean in Newfoundland and planned on doing the same in the Pacific Ocean when he reached the other side of Canada in British Columbia. He decided to finish the run or die trying.

After 143 days of running, covering a distance of 5,373 kilometers, or 3,339 miles (that's about equivalent to running a marathon each day), it was discovered that cancer had spread to both his lungs, and he was forced to stop his run. Nine months later, Terry died trying. But his legacy lives on.

I recently read a statistic that more than $400 million has been raised in Terry's name as a result of his decision to raise money for cancer research. That's remarkable considering that when he started the run, Terry was only raising a few dollars per day.

Can you imagine what it was like standing in Terry Fox's place as he told his family, friends, and doctors what he had decided to do? Can you imagine what responses he would have received? I wonder how many people told him his dream wasn't realistic.

I'm positive that his family, friends, and especially his doctors, jumped up right away and began telling him of the obstacles he would face—weather, fatigue, pain, the threat of cancer spreading, and the fact that he had only one leg.

Did Terry fear the same? It's possible. Did he ever take his eye off the goal? I don't think so. Terry Fox made a decision to do something that many people deemed impossible. He decided to do it and decided not to focus on the obstacles, but to focus and stay focused on the goal, and through those decisions, he was able to change the world.

Changing the world doesn't always mean raising hundreds of millions for cancer research like Terry Fox did. So what will you do? What will you do this weekend? This month? This year? How will you leave a legacy?

Yeah, *Make Your Own Lunch* is about having a ton of fun, but as you're going along having incredible adventures, remember to leave something behind for the people coming after you. Decide to leave your legacy.

16

FOOD GROUP IV

Decide who you will be.

→ I played basketball as a sophomore, and there was nothing more important to me than a new pair of basketball shoes. I was lucky enough to have a decent part-time job so I could afford to buy a new pair of basketball shoes every five or six months.

One day, I made my way to the local mall and searched sports stores for a pair I liked and that fell in my price range. I hit up the first store and found the perfect pair. I looked around, and nobody came over to ask me if I needed help or if I wanted to try on a size. A little angry, I put the shoe back on the shelf and decided I would take my business somewhere else.

In the next store, the same thing happened. I picked my shoes off the shelf and looked around at the store staff joking around while they had a dunk competition using a children's basketball net over the change room door.

Feeling angrier than before, I put the shoe back on the shelf and stormed out of the store to the last sports store in my hometown mall. I walked in, still pretty angry about the whole shopping experience, and found the same pair of shoes. I took it off the rack and looked over my shoulder at the only employee as she talked on the phone to her friend about her weekend plans. She stared at me for a second, then turned her back to me as she continued the conversation.

I couldn't believe it.

I actually slammed the shoe back on the rack as

I stomped my way out of the store, out of the mall, into my car, and drove back to my parents' house. When I got back home, I threw the front door open and stormed into the kitchen where my mom was making dinner. I told her what had just happened at the mall as I paced between the kitchen and living room.

"Nobody respects kids these days! They don't think I have money? I probably make twice as much as them at my part-time job! Do they even know the business they just lost? I'll tell all of my friends never to shop at those places. I'm going to write a letter to their head office."

Somebody was lucky I didn't have Twitter then.

As I ranted and raved to my mom and paced back and forth from the kitchen to the living room, I walked past a giant mirror and stopped midsentence. I saw myself. I saw my baggy jeans tucked into my Timberland boots and giant hooded sweater with the hood pulled up over my New York Yankees hat that sat low enough on my head that you couldn't see my eyes. I saw myself and something became clear to me.

Now what I'm about to write, I don't agree with. In fact, I *hate* it. However, I think it needs to be said: the world judges you.

The world judges you on a million different things—how you dress, how you walk, the music you listen to, the people you hang around with, how you talk, where you work, who your family is, what kind of car you drive, how you dance, who you date, how you do your hair, how you drive, what you drink, your skin color, the church you go to, what you eat, how much you eat, and a million other things.

The world will always judge you. And it sucks! And guess what? If you don't show and tell people who you are, they will treat you how they think they should treat you on the basis of the things they've seen or heard. Nobody approached me that day in the mall because I didn't look approachable. They probably thought I was in there to steal something and were waiting to call the cops. And because I didn't show them how to treat me, they treated me how they thought they should treat me.

If you don't show and tell people who you are, they will treat you how they think they should treat you, and they will be wrong!

By no means am I saying you can't wear what you want to wear or listen to the music you want to listen to. That day in my parents' kitchen, I made a decision. I didn't change the way I dressed or how I walked. I didn't change the way I wore my hat or the music I listened to. I changed what I was showing and telling people about who I was.

IF YOU DON'T SHOW AND TELL PEOPLE WHO YOU ARE, THEY WILL TREAT YOU HOW THEY THINK THEY SHOULD TREAT YOU, AND THEY WILL BE WRONG!

Now when I go into a store, I go in with a smile on my face, I make eye contact, and I ask the people working how their day is going. And if I need to try something on or need a different color, size, or style, I ask. I don't give them a chance to assume something about me. I show and tell the people in stores that I am approachable. I show and tell them how to treat me.

When I first started in business, I came across the same thing. I was young with zero experience, and a bunch of people were trying to judge me on the basis of my age and lack of experience. When I first walked in to meetings, I could see people judging me, discounting my abilities because of my age or that I was wearing bright red sneakers. Their opinions changed, though, as soon as I spoke. I shattered their assumptions and judgments by showing them that I wasn't who they thought I was.

You see, *you* get to decide who *you* will be. There's no destiny; there's no luck. There's you, and there's your decisions.

What type of person do you want to be? Do you want to be happy? What do happy people do? Start doing that! How do happy people act? Start acting like that! What do happy people talk about? Start doing the same thing.

I have one warning. Once you've decided who you want to be, be that person.

Don't cop out. Don't have a part-time personality. Be that person all the time. Don't do it just to get what you want then go back to being the old you. You are not who people tell you you are. You aren't clumsy because your dad has been telling you that you're clumsy your entire life. You aren't ugly or fat because your boyfriend is always making jokes about you. If you think you are those things, then it's because you've decided to listen to, and believe, those people.

Do you want people to think you're beautiful? Show and tell people that you are beautiful! Do things that make you feel beautiful. Who cares if you aren't on the cover of a fashion magazine or don't look like the person who is? Smile more. Show people you are confident.

Who are you? Who do you want to become? What can you do to start showing people that's who you are? Are you being treated the way you want to be treated?

I hear from so many students who say things like, "I am sick and tired of my parents treating me like _____." Or, "My boyfriend is always treating me like _____."

I am sick and tired of them being sick and tired.

If your parents aren't treating you the way you want, show and tell them how to treat you. If your boyfriend or girlfriend isn't treating you right, show and tell him or her how you want to be treated. Show and tell people who you are and how they should treat you.

Keep in mind that there may be times where you clearly show and tell people how to treat you and they won't get it. People are complex. Everybody has their own issues, and sometimes people are completely unable to change their behavior. And that's OK, if you decide it's OK.

If people aren't able to treat you the way that you are asking them to treat you, then it's up to you to decide what type of relationship you will have with those people.

You are smart, you are creative, and you deserve respect. You may be young, but that has nothing to do with the value you have. Don't ever let people discount you and your talents on the basis of your age, religion, skin color, weight, or appearance. Decide who you will be, and show and tell people that's who you are.

IF PEOPLE AREN'T ABLE TO TREAT YOU THE WAY THAT YOU ARE ASKING THEM TO TREAT YOU, THEN IT'S UP TO YOU TO DECIDE WHAT TYPE OF RELATIONSHIP YOU WILL HAVE WITH THOSE PEOPLE.

STEP 4

EAT UP! (A.K.A. CHEW, DIGEST, REPEAT)

17

RECOMMENDED DAILY INTAKE I: VISION

Create a vision for your epic life and administer a daily dose of your dreams.

I ALWAYS HAD A PASSION FOR FLASHIN'. BEFORE I HAD IT I CLOSED MY EYES AND IMAGINED.

—KANYE WEST, "GOOD LIFE"

In my junior year of high school, I took a class called Personal Life Management. It was a terrible class for me. The teacher gave us an assignment one day where we had to write down our goals for the following five years. Once we handed it in, the teacher was going to review our goals and grade them on the basis of how realistic they were. She even taught us an acronym to help us set our goals, SMART:

S — Specific

M — Measurable

A — Attainable

R — Realistic

T — Timely

The student who handed in a nicely typed assignment stating that his or her goal was to finish high school, go to college, then get certified to become a teacher — that student got an A. The teacher felt that it was completely realistic for someone to live that life. Why? Because it was the teacher's life! That's what our teacher knew as realistic.

The student who came in and had the goal of becoming a rock star got an F. Why? Because there's no way anyone from Ajax, Ontario, Canada, could ever be a rock star. And the student who wanted to cure cancer? He had to speak with the teacher after class about more realistic goal setting.

I handed in an assignment that went something like this:

I want to wake up sometime in the next five years in my dream house, a five-thousand-square-foot mansion with a basketball court in the backyard and enough room for my dog to run around without me ever having to stoop and scoop! I want my dream car in the driveway with a motorcycle in the garage, both gassed up and ready to take me anywhere I want to go. I want to travel first-class to my vacation homes in Hawaii and Japan. I want to take four months off every year for vacations and traveling. I want my businesses to do well enough that at age forty, I can choose when I will work and what I will do.

Ryan, wake up!

That's what you're thinking, isn't it? Maybe you aren't thinking *wake up*, but I can almost guarantee that you believe this life isn't realistic. Or maybe you think this type of life is only realistic for other people, but not for you and me. Am I right?

Why is it that any time you try to talk about your dreams and goals for the future, people tell you to be realistic? Or even worse, why is it that when you're dreaming about your future, you end up telling yourself that the things you want aren't realistic?

You're probably like the millions of other people who have been taught that life has to follow a set plan. You have to go to high school, then go to college, then get a job, get married, have kids, and eventually retire, hopefully with enough money to visit Florida once a year.

You are going to hear it a million times as you continue living an epic life: "be realistic." For some reason, being an accountant, a teacher, an electrician, or a lawyer is realistic to most people. But being a young adult who is happy and working on a career that you love on your terms and living the life of your dreams is not realistic.

The life I just explained to you, the life I want, is somebody's life! There are people who wake up every day in their dream houses, married to their dream spouses. They take their dream vacations, drive their dream cars, and work in a career they have dreamed about. They went to their dream schools, and they are doing all of the things they have dreamed of.

This isn't even about being rich or famous (but it could be, if that's what you want). This is about making real decisions about what you are going to do to live epically.

Why aren't these things realistic for you? Or are they? And why is it that the same people who told you that you could do anything are the same people telling you that the life you want isn't realistic? Does that make sense?

THIS ISN'T EVEN ABOUT BEING RICH OR FAMOUS (BUT IT COULD BE, IF THAT'S WHAT YOU WANT). THIS IS ABOUT MAKING REAL DECISIONS ABOUT WHAT YOU ARE GOING TO DO TO LIVE EPICALLY.

The following are some ways that people try to tell you your dreams aren't realistic:

- "It's nice to dream, but you eventually have to get real."
- "OK, that sounds nice, but you should really have a backup plan."
- "What are you going to do when that doesn't work?"
- "I don't think anyone has done that before."
- "I think you should have a plan B."
- "Don't you think you should come up with a realistic plan?"
- "People like us don't do stuff like that."
- "If it was that easy, then everyone would be doing it!"
- "Life isn't easy."
- "Maybe you should try something not so difficult."

And there are so many more excuses.

Listen, a lot of the time, the people who are telling you to "be realistic" are telling you that because they care about you, and they don't want to see you hurt, disappointed, or let down. But *some* of the people who tell you to be realistic tell you that because at some point in their life, they probably stopped chasing their dreams and settled for the life they currently have. And now they believe it isn't realistic for other people to live their dreams because they gave up on theirs.

The people telling you to have a plan B usually tell you that because they are living *their* plan B or plan C.

And I am not, for a *second*, saying that the people around you giving advice and guidance, like your parents and teachers, aren't living their exact dream lives. I'm just saying that the ones who are will never tell you to "be realistic." You can usually tell who is living the way they want by the way they give you advice about your plans.

The people who live their dreams, do the things they want, drive the cars they want, surround themselves with great friends and family, work the jobs they have dreamed about, and live a life they love always give the same advice: "You can do anything you put your mind to!" or "Never stop dreaming. The sky's the limit!" or "If I can do it, you can too!"

Everyone at my high school found out just how realistic it was to become a rock star when four guys from our school got together to form a little band called Sum 41. For those of you who don't know, they are a multiplatinum, chart-topping, award-winning rock band.

Here's the coolest part about things that are realistic: reality isn't permanent.

Each day, new realities show up and old realities disappear. On a snowy day, snowboarding, for some people, is a reality. On a rainy day in August, snowboarding may not be a reality, unless you're willing to jump on a plane and head somewhere with snow. You decide.

At this very minute, you may feel like the things you want are not part of your reality. You are about to change that.

For some people, waking up and heading to work in sneakers and a T-shirt would get them fired. For others, it's what they wear pretty much every day to the office.

I have friends who have decided that their reality will be teaching seminars about beer in Japan or teaching scuba diving in Honduras and Mexico. My friend Nick's reality includes hanging out with rock stars, filming music videos every day. I know people who travel the globe performing for packed venues. The girl I met in Guatemala, Leila, her reality is traveling the globe and writing about her adventures. Paul Munro's reality is running a nonprofit that designs awesome skateboards and gives them to children in developing countries.

If I told my Personal Life Management teacher that I was going to work a job

AT THIS VERY MINUTE, YOU MAY FEEL LIKE THE THINGS YOU WANT ARE NOT PART OF YOUR REALITY. YOU ARE ABOUT TO CHANGE THAT.

where people pay for my flights all over North America and then pay me to speak and tell stories about my life, I can only imagine what she would have said.

The people who are living their dreams know that it's possible to do those things, and they are usually passionate about telling others to shoot for the stars. They know they decide their own reality. They know they make their own lunch.

Your Recommended Daily Intake is all about getting a daily dose of your dreams and deciding that they are realistic! See those things every day. Forget plan B. Forget what other people say is or isn't realistic. Decide for yourself what your reality looks like.

➔ Monday morning rolled along and our all-male gym class was standing around waiting for our self-defense instructor to join us. I had no idea how my life was about to change.

Our class was required to spend a week learning basic self-defense, and I was excited to see who would be teaching us the choke holds, kicks, and tiger uppercuts that I had seen in video games. As the doors opened and our self-defense instructor came in, I laughed out loud. Our self-defense instructor was a five-foot-one, hundred-pound woman. In my fifteen-year-old mind, I thought, "What in the world can this little *woman* teach me, a sports god, about defending myself?" (I can promise you that my thoughts have drastically changed since then.)

That Monday morning, I decided that she had nothing valuable to teach me, and instead of listening to her instructions, I would make her week with us as difficult as possible. Any time she demonstrated something or explained a concept to the class, I cracked a joke and disrupted the lesson.

Four days passed and it was Friday, which was the last day of the self-defense course. It started out like every other class. We stood in a circle as she explained what we were going to do that day. I was hardly listening and had my back turned to her as I joked with my basketball buddies. She asked for a volunteer, but I wasn't paying attention, until I heard her say, "You!" I turned around to see her finger pointing in my face. She then said, "You've been a class clown all week and made things really difficult. You're my volunteer!"

I was still trying to crack jokes. "That kind of defeats the purpose of a volunteer—" I wasn't able to finish my sentence, because she grabbed me by my shirt and dragged me into the middle of the class circle. The class was laughing but quickly shut up when she shouted, "Punch me!"

"Umm…" I cleared my throat. "Pardon me?" I asked, trying to clarify what I just heard.

"Punch me!"

"Miss, I can't punch you. I'm a guy. You're a girl. I will hurt you, maybe even *kill* you. Besides, my mom told me to never hit a girl."

She started to get angry. "I have been hit by guys twice your strength and twice your size. Now I want you to punch me!"

I looked around the room, then I got into my fighting stance, made a fist, closed my eyes, and with all my power, I swung a punch.

That's where I black out.

When I regained consciousness, I was lying facedown on the wrestling mats, about ten feet from where I remembered standing. She had her hand in my hair, dragging me by my head around the circle as the class laughed hysterically. She pulled me to the middle of the circle, jerked me to my feet by my head, and then said something I will never forget: "Do you want to know how to win a fight every time, with anybody? Get control of the head! If you get control of the head, you win, because wherever the head goes the body has to follow!"

She demonstrated for ten minutes how she could throw me anywhere she wanted because she controlled my head. She made me stand up by jerking my hair up. She made me lie down by jerking my hair down. She made me look like an idiot by doing all of this.

I learned one of life's most important lessons that day—where the head goes, the body follows.

Reality is for those who lack imagination. —Lily Tomlin

WHERE THE HEAD GOES, THE BODY FOLLOWS.

Where's Your Head At?

When I work with students and ask them to tell me what their dream life looks like, many of them respond by saying, "What's the point?" or "I can't do that, I can't go there, I can't have that," or "I can't become that."

I tell them, "Where the head goes, the body has to follow!" What I mean is, what do you spend your time thinking about? Who do you spend your time with? What do you spend your time doing? What do you spend your time talking about? Where do you spend your time? These things, and many others, determine where you will go, what you will do, and who you will become.

Today is your head, and tomorrow and every other day that follows is your body. You're not just going to wake up one day in the life you dream about. You start by thinking about those things, talking about those places, finding people who want to do the same things as you, and then you start doing it!

When you want something, decide that it's real and then place your order. Tell life what to give you. Imagine what your life could be like. See, touch, taste, smell, and feel your dream life. The more you do this and decide it's real for you, the more likely it is that you will find ways to make it happen. Decide it's real and then decide to focus on it every day. Start pulling or even jerking your head (your thoughts and actions today) in the right direction so that your body (your future) can be where you want it to be.

I know that some situations aren't as perfect as you want them to be. I know that right now, you might feel trapped in your life and current situation, but trust me—it will get better once you decide it *can* get better and that it's *realistic* for you to make it better.

If you get control of the head, you've won, because where the head goes, the body has to follow.

Where's *your* head at?

Oh yeah, and when you're thinking about this kind of stuff, forget what you don't want. Focus on what you do want…*all* of it.

Place Your Order

After a long day of traveling, I arrived in Bratislava, Slovakia, tired, smelly, and hungry enough to reclassify my own fingers as Vienna party sausages. I was in a rush to catch a train that was waiting outside of the station, but I couldn't resist stopping at a café as I was running through the terminal.

The lady who worked there had her back turned to me. As I was about to say, "Excuse me," the woman turned around and had me fearing for my life.

She had a full beard.

She didn't speak any English, so I immediately started speaking tourist English.

"Me. Ham and cheese sandwich. No tomatoes. No onion. No mustard. No sauerkraut. Only lettuce, green peppers, and cheese."

I placed my order and then hopped over to the money exchange counter to get some local currency while she made my sandwich. When I got back to the café, I saw my sandwich sitting on a plate on top of the counter. I started the mime game again while telling her, "No. This is to go. To go…To go…? To *goooo*. *Tooooo goooooo*."

She lifted the sandwich off the plate, pushed it aside, slammed the sandwich on the counter, wrapped it, and told me to go. I took the sandwich and went running to my train that was about to depart.

As I sat down on the train with my friend, I took a huge bite of the sandwich and almost puked. The only things I tasted were tomatoes, onions, mustard, and sauerkraut—all the things I had told the mysterious bearded woman *not* to put on the sandwich.

Spitting the sandwich into a napkin, I started complaining.

"I guess nobody in this stupid country speaks English? That woman couldn't even get a simple order right."

My friend cut me off. "Obviously she understands a little bit of English because you got exactly what you didn't want."

I stared at her like she had just told me that Bigfoot and the tooth fairy are the same person.

"She only heard the words tomatoes, mustard, onions, and sauerkraut, so that's what you got. You should've told her what you wanted, and only what you wanted."

She was right.

Your brain is a bearded Slovakian woman, and if you don't tell it what you *do* want, you'll get what you *don't* want. So many times when we're trying to make decisions about what we want to have, where we want to go, what we want to do, and who we want to be, we start by listing all of the things we don't want.

Stop wasting your time!

You would never go into a restaurant and order by telling the server the things you *don't* want; you tell them exactly what you do want.

"Hello. I don't want the cheeseburger or the chicken wrap. I don't want the soup or salad. I definitely don't want the quesadillas, and I don't want the mashed potatoes. I don't want the chicken wings. I really don't want the baby-back ribs, either..."

Do you see what I am getting at?

This is why people tell secrets that somebody told them *not* to share. It's why you dropped your books in the hall when you thought, *Don't drop your books*. It's why your face went red as a tomato when you thought, *Don't blush*, and it's also why you're late when you think, *Don't be late today*.

Change the way you talk to yourself and others. Place your order! Start telling your friends, your family, your life, and most important, yourself what you want. Start placing your order. If you don't, just like in a restaurant, you will get what you didn't want, or even worse, you won't get anything at all.

If you want to remember someone's name, tell yourself to remember it. If you don't want to be late, tell yourself to be early.

Your Recommended Daily Intake of vision can be one of the most exciting parts of making your own lunch. You literally get to decide anything you want. You get to decide what's real for your life and your future. You get to start pulling your head in the direction of the things you truly want. You get to place your order and get exactly what you want.

YOUR BRAIN IS A BEARDED SLOVAKIAN WOMAN, AND IF YOU DON'T TELL IT WHAT YOU *DO* WANT, YOU'LL GET WHAT YOU *DON'T* WANT.

18

RECOMMENDED DAILY INTAKE II: ACTION

How to come up with an action plan and then actually act on it.

SEEING WHAT YOU WANT IS AMAZINGLY IMPORTANT, BUT THE MOST IMPORTANT THING YOU CAN DO IS TO START MAKING MOVES TO GET THAT STUFF, GO TO THOSE PLACES, DO THAT STUFF, AND BECOME THAT PERSON.

→ Two years after I returned to Canada from Japan, the traveling bug bit me again. I borrowed my little brother's backpack and bought a plane ticket to Frankfurt, Germany. I decided I would spend the summer backpacking through different parts of Europe. I started in Germany, then headed to Slovakia. From Slovakia, I went to Austria and the Czech Republic, and eventually I made my way to France and flew home from Paris.

While I was walking around Prague, I came across an amazing Gothic-style cathedral with a soaring bell tower. From the ground, I saw a group of tourists at the top who were excited to have reached the top of the bell tower. I thought to myself, "Either they're giving away free Justin Bieber tickets up there or the view is just *that* good." I decided I wanted to get up there to take some pictures and see what everyone was so excited about.

I walked into the church and began looking for the staircase leading to the top of the tower. I fully expected to find a wide-open staircase, or maybe even an elevator with a sign that would say, "The easy way up to the greatest view in Europe." Yeah, that didn't exist.

After a few minutes of searching with no luck, I finally asked a worker in the church if he could show me the staircase. With a smile on his face (the kind of smile that says "you idiot"—the same smile your mom gives you when she tells you

you're special), he pointed to a small dark hole in the wall. He grabbed my arm and guided me to the small entrance, and after giving me a thumbs-up, he left me to find my way up.

I definitely thought the worker didn't understand my English, and I had no idea why I was standing in front of the small entrance. I looked into the hole in the wall and saw a staircase. The stairs were nothing like I had imagined. They were wrapped around a single pole. They were so tightly wrapped around the pole that you could only see four stairs at a time, because after the fourth step, they started to wrap around. The staircase was about one and a half feet wide, and there wasn't enough room for me to stand up straight. The staircase wasn't even big enough for me to go up by myself, and for some crazy Czech Republic reason, they had people going up and down at the same time!

This would be a good point of the story to tell you that at that time, I was both severely claustrophobic and deathly scared of heights. (Both of which I have since conquered!) Entering the dark hole, I felt the panic take over my body. My legs started shaking, and my heart started beating like it was attacking my rib cage to get out of my chest. I knew I wanted to see the city from the top of the tower and that I may never have the chance again. I was almost ready to back out, but as I turned around to leave, there was an old Italian woman standing behind me. She looked right in my eyes and said in her Super Mario–like voice, "Go, skinny boy. It's so easy." She was kind of right. I took her advice and walked back into the dark entrance. I took a deep breath, looked to the floor, and took the first step. Then a miracle happened: another step appeared.

So I took the next step, and again another one appeared. I took that one and the one after that.

More than 290 steps and seven gallons of sweat later, I reached the top and was exposed to the most amazing view of Prague. Sure, I smelled like a Whopper Jr. with extra onions, but the houses, the scenery, and the view were perfect. It was more than I had expected, and it was one of my most epic moments in Europe.

I am so glad I decided to take that first step. I realized why the group of tourists before me was so excited. No Justin Bieber tickets, just an awesome view of one of the greatest cities in Europe. If I never took that first step, I would have never experienced that moment. I literally conquered the bell tower step by step.

Sitting at the top of that bell tower, I realized two important lessons. One, never leave home without putting on extra-strength deodorant, and two, more important, all you can ever do is take the next step. A quote from Martin Luther

King Jr. flickered in my head, and I found myself smiling at the lesson I had just learned. I finally realized what he was talking about. (And he wasn't talking about a cathedral in Prague!)

Take the first step in faith. You don't have to see the whole staircase, just take the first step.—Martin Luther King Jr.

If you tell yourself that something is a really big deal, and that it's going to be hard, and that it's not going to be fun, then chances are that's exactly what it will be like. But if you spend your time thinking about how great it could be and how much fun you will have, you will find yourself looking for ways to make it easier.

How to Start Anything

OK, let's walk through an example of how to get started on something you want to do.

Like I learned in Prague, it's great to know that the top of the tower is there (your goal), but there are a bunch of steps you need to take to get there.

Let's say that you want to move to Japan to teach English for a year. How could you begin taking the actions needed to make it a reality?

1. **Make a list.** Make a list of all the steps you think you would need to take to make your move to Japan happen. Don't worry about the order, just list everything out on a piece of paper, in a Word document, or on the back of a napkin.

2. **Get organized.** Organize your list into the order you think things need to

be done. Start with all the small, easy, quick goals and then work your way into the harder stuff.

3. **Make a commitment.** Commit to your plan and share it with somebody. This could mean telling your best friend what you want to do and how you're going to do it, or it could mean starting a blog or a YouTube channel to document the process from start to finish.

4. **Do it.** Get something done right now. There is without a doubt something you could be doing *right now* to get started. It may be something as simple as finding people on social media who are talking about Japan, or maybe you could email a blogger who's been writing about life in Japan as an English teacher.

5. **Keep moving.** Start crossing stuff off the list. As you reach your steps or goals, cross them off, delete them, mark them as complete. Make an update to your blog or tell your friends or family how things are going, and ask for help when you need it.

The people who live the lives they want are able to do so because they constantly tell themselves it's realistic, and they search for ways to make it happen. They've seen the top of their bell tower, and they are taking all of the steps they need to take to reach it.

I am not going to pretend like it's always going to be easy, but I *am* going to act like it is worth it and very realistic.

I want you to constantly see what it is you want, because there are going to be times when you will question whether it's worth the work, and the only thing that'll keep you going is that vision and the actions you are taking toward achieving that vision.

The things you want in your life, the person you want to become, and the places you want to go don't happen by accident. If you haven't picked up on it yet, let me make it clear again: this is going to require some action on your part. Your dream car isn't going to park itself in your driveway. Your relationship with your parents isn't going to automatically get better. The boss of your dream job isn't going to randomly pick your name out of the phonebook, call you up, and offer you a job. The girl or guy you can't stop thinking about probably isn't going to just send you a love letter without you taking some action first.

Two guys named Orville and Wilbur are the perfect example of getting your Recommended Daily Intake of action.

The Wright brothers started off by thinking about flight, deciding it was real,

If we only undertake little things, it only gives us the power for little things, but if we try to do great things in a great way, it gives us all the power there is.

—Wallace Wattles, *The Science of Being Great*

and deciding they would achieve it. They didn't stop there and kick their feet up, spending their days merely dreaming about it and waiting for an airplane to magically appear in their workshop. They took action. Day by day, they formulated a plan. They sketched designs, built prototypes, tested engines, and studied flight. They began piecing their dream together, step by step, action by action. They knew it was real for them to fly in an airplane, and they decided they would be the ones to do it. Not once did they think, "Wait, maybe this is impossible." They stuck to their vision and took every step until it was real.

You know the result of their hard work. If you don't know, just stare at the sky for an hour and I bet you will see the product of their thoughts, actions, and decisions.

Sometimes you have dreams, stuff you want to do, places you want to go, and things you want in your life, but it seems like too much. The amount of work can seem too hard; so many people look at where they are and where they want to go and assume they'll never make it, and they give up before taking the first step:

You want to become a rock star but think it's impossible.

You want to go to college but don't have the grades.

You want to be a successful millionaire but don't even have a bank account.

You want to travel to Tahiti but can't even find it on a globe.

You want to go scuba diving but are afraid of the water.

You want to do what you want but are afraid to tell your family.

When I was standing at the foot of the bell tower, I made a decision to only look at the next step. I told myself not to look up or down, but to focus completely on the next step, because I knew that if I could make it to the next step, another one would appear. I knew that the top of the tower was at the top, where I saw it, and I knew that I would eventually make it if I could just take the next step and the one after that.

Once you've decided what you want, and decided that it's real, take a step. It doesn't have to be a giant step, it just has to be *a* step, the next step, and maybe it's the first step.

Sometimes making these decisions and working toward the things you want can feel like a black hole, and sometimes you won't know all the steps to take. Sometimes you'll need somebody to guide you to the staircase, but all you can ever take is the next step. Don't be one of those people who get completely overwhelmed looking at what they want and thinking that it's too far away.

Take a little bit of time to understand exactly what you're looking at. Look at

If we worked on the assumption that what is accepted as true really is true, then there would be little hope for advance.
—Orville Wright

your next step. Understand its shape, its height, and its size. If you think I'm really talking about an actual staircase, now might be a good time for a break, or better yet, a nap—or a trip to your doctor's office.

Don't give up before you even begin. Focus on the next step. Be that person who is determined to have what he or she wants, and then the next step will seem so small in relation to the stuff you are climbing for. Be one of those people who thinks like the old Italian lady behind me: "Go, skinny boy. It's so easy!"

That trip to Central America, the Harley-Davidson you want, the full-ride scholarship to Michigan State University, your pilot's license, and all of your other epic adventures are like a bell tower. There is a top and a bunch of steps in between. All you can do is take the next step until you eventually reach the top.

I know it's a little overwhelming trying to conquer your world and live the life you want all at once. It's super important for you to chop things into bite-sized pieces.

Bite-Sized Pieces

If you sat down to dinner in a restaurant and the server brought you a giant steak, you would never jam it into your mouth without using a knife and fork. That's rude.

ONCE YOU'VE DECIDED WHAT YOU WANT, AND DECIDED THAT IT'S REAL, TAKE A STEP. IT DOESN'T HAVE TO BE A GIANT STEP, IT JUST HAS TO BE *A* STEP, THE NEXT STEP, AND MAYBE IT'S THE FIRST STEP.

My mom would make you sit in the corner for a time-out. You would cry, and my older brother Dan would make fun of you and most likely throw things at you. You would then cry more. Welcome to my childhood.

You would never stuff that steak into your mouth without cutting it up into smaller bite-sized pieces that you could manage, and then piece by piece, you would eat your meal.

Ask yourself, "Am I trying to jam my dreams into my life without cutting them into bite-sized pieces first? Am I trying to get to the top of my bell tower without taking the steps I *need* to take?"

Once you've taken that first step, it's time to start looking toward your destination and the best course of action to get there. You won't always know all the steps. And that's OK. Just start with what you do know. What do the steps look like? About how many steps are there? Are there twists and turns? Lists, like directions, are a great way to start navigating toward a destination. Don't get hung up on the order in which things need to be done.

Sometimes different steps appear. Some steps can change. Some steps may even disappear. All you can ever do is take the next step and keep moving forward. Step by step, dot by dot, and piece by piece, you can do the things you strive for.

I saw myself writing this book, I saw people reading it, I decided that it was completely realistic for me to write it, and then I just started writing it. I have never taken a writing class. I'm not a grammar expert. I still struggle with spelling, and I still don't know if it's *there*, *their*, or *they're*. My editor, Suzy, will tell you that I literally use the word *literally* a thousand times a day and am literally wrong literally every time.

I started by listing the stories I wanted to tell, the things I wanted to write about. Then I listed the order of the chapters and eventually started looking for editors and publishing options. Step by step and piece by piece, this book has come together.

Why is it important not to get caught up in planning every step? Because the path will change. There will be times where you will need to switch to your path B or C, D, E, F, or G.

If it's a trip to Paris you want, what are some things you could do today to bring you closer to being there? List everything and anything you could do to help you get to Paris, then step by step, piece by piece, start putting it together. Don't worry if you don't have every action figured out. You will constantly have new ideas once you get started. You could start reading a guidebook that recommends a great hostel and then realize you need to research hostels. That's another action to add to the list.

Things will happen a lot quicker than you think because you will constantly be crossing things off your to-do list. You will constantly be taking steps. Take the time to figure out how you can cut your vision into bite-sized pieces. What can you do today to bring you closer to the things you want? Start by getting a daily dose of your dreams and let that lead to your Recommended Daily Intake of action. Take a deep breath and take the first step. I promise another one will appear.

19

IT DOESN'T ALWAYS TASTE GOOD

Everybody has obstacles—not everybody will move past them, but you can.

KITCHENS CATCH ON FIRE, CHICKEN DOESN'T GET COOKED, POTS BOIL OVER, YOUR DAD FORGETS TO TURN THE OVEN ON FOR THANKSGIVING DINNER, AND YOUR GRANDMA DROPS HER DENTURES IN THE BIRTHDAY CAKE. EVEN WHEN YOU'RE FOLLOWING THE RECIPE PERFECTLY, SOMETIMES THINGS DON'T WORK OUT AS YOU PLANNED.

What I'm about to share with you is something I don't tell very many people, but I wanted to share it in this book. It is something even most of my closest friends haven't heard. Welcome to my circle of trust.

Riding home from work one night on a packed train in Tokyo, with only a few weeks left on my contract in Japan, I had a panic attack. I didn't know it at the time, but it was a panic attack. Not like a figure-of-speech panic attack. I mean an attack that felt like a heart attack. I couldn't breathe, my chest tightened up, I was sweating, my heart was pounding, my vision became blurry, and it felt like I was actually dying. No joke.

I stumbled off the train at a random train station and collapsed on a bench on the platform. I had never been more frightened in my life. I had no idea what was happening and couldn't speak enough Japanese to ask for help or explain what was going on. After about fifteen minutes, it passed. I assumed I had eaten something bad or had the flu.

The next night, while I was teaching a lesson to my Japanese students, the same thing happened. It was so bad I had to leave the classroom and ended up blacking out in the teachers' prep room. I had no idea what was happening or what was wrong.

The next morning, I didn't go to work. My stomach was insanely tight. I could hardly breathe and didn't feel like moving a single muscle. My girlfriend at the time came to my house and booked a doctor's appointment for me, and then she came along to translate. She explained the symptoms to him, and he thought maybe it was the flu. The doc gave me, like, seventeen different medications and sent me on my way.

It didn't get better. In fact, it got worse. I called in sick three days in a row, which became seven days, and then eleven days, and with only one week left on my contract, I called my branch manager and informed him I would be going back to Canada early to figure out what was wrong with me and wouldn't be able to work my remaining five shifts.

For six months after returning from Japan, I had panic attacks. Daily.

One time driving to the airport to pick up my friend, who was visiting from Japan, I had to pull over on the side of the highway because I felt like I was going to pass out. I never talked about it. I told everybody I was just feeling a little sick. I wasn't hanging out with my friends. When I did go out, I went home early because I didn't want to have a panic attack in public. Being in most public places would make me feel sick, and I would start to have panic attacks. At the time, I had no idea what was going on. I thought I was way too young to have panic attacks or to feel that much stress.

Then one day while surfing the Internet trying to figure out what was wrong with me, I found a forum discussing panic attacks, stress, and anxiety. That's when I found out what was going on. But how could I, at age twenty-three, be suffering from stress? It turns out that there was a lot of stuff adding up to cause a lot of stress in my life. I had made so many decisions about my life while in Japan: decisions about the types of people and stuff I would allow into my life. Decisions about the things I wanted to do, places I wanted to go, and the person I wanted to become. Things were supposed to be perfect when I got home.

I was supposed to start a business, make a lot of money, and do all these amazing things, but that was kind of impossible, considering I couldn't leave the house most days. I started reading about anxiety and stress and looking at the symptoms as well as the experiences other people were having. That's when things started getting better. It's like as soon as I knew what was happening, I was able to see it before it happened. I was able to see what things triggered it and how I could prevent it.

It was exactly like that strange noise you hear while having a sleepover at your friend's house. It's so scary the first time you hear it. You can't figure out what it is. Maybe it's a ghost. Maybe somebody broke in the house to steal your Xbox games. After listening carefully and inspecting the noise with a flashlight, you realize that it was just the wind blowing branches against the window. That noise isn't scary anymore. You fall asleep without any problems. And the next time you sleep over, the noise doesn't faze you at all.

These panic attacks were just like that. But they were still happening from time to time. Then one day, I had an experience that changed it all.

My business had been up and running for some time, and my speaking career was just picking up. I had been speaking mainly in classrooms to small audiences, but I eventually got the opportunity to get on a big stage in front of more than a thousand students. I remember waiting backstage, and the panic started about ten minutes before I was supposed to go on. All these questions started running through my mind:

What if I suck?
What if I puke onstage?
What if I pass out?
What if they hate me?
What if I'm not funny?

Then I heard the words, "Please welcome our guest speaker, Ryan Porter." The crowd started cheering. I walked out onstage, started talking, and then something remarkable happened. Well, actually, nothing happened. That's just it. Nothing happened. That's when it all disappeared. My stomach loosened, my head cleared, the shaking stopped, and I rocked the stage.

In my hotel room later that night, I felt like a million pounds had been lifted from my shoulders. I was so relieved. That's when I realized how to overcome the stress, the anxiety, and panic: stop thinking about the stress, anxiety, and panic. Where your head goes, the body has to follow.

So that's how I overcame it. I didn't focus on it. If I felt stress coming on, I thought about what I needed to be doing to bring me closer to the things I had decided to get, the places I had decided to go, the stuff I had decided to do, and the person I had decided to be. And like magic, it all went away.

It's been years since I've felt that type of anxiety; it feels really good to write it here. I was so afraid to talk about it before, because I thought if people knew, they would think I was weak, or unstable, or depressed, when that wasn't the case at all.

I'm sure it's happened to you before. You have this plan in your head about how something should work out. You know that you're doing what you should be doing but then…*Bam!* A giant obstacle lands in your way.

That obstacle might be a sickness or it might have something to do with money or lack of it. It might have to do with abuse, the death of a loved one, or loneliness. It might be self-doubt or lack of confidence or fear of rejection. That obstacle might be something you've never dealt with or something that none of your friends or family have dealt with. That's OK.

You are not alone.

→ I jumped off the ferry and landed on a dock packed with people shouting at me in Spanish and English. I was stoked to be on the island of Utila in Honduras. I had decided to take a month off in the summer of 2009 to backpack around Central America.

I went to Utila with one purpose: to get my scuba-diving license. I don't know why, but I have this weird thing with water. I love being in it, especially under it. I think my parents adopted me from a herd of manatees.

On my first day at the scuba school I had signed up for, we sat in a classroom learning the basics of diving, equipment, and safety. As we sat around watching safety videos and reading our textbooks, our instructor, Frank—not your uncle Frank—asked the class, "What's the most dangerous thing in the water? The thing that will most likely hurt you or kill you?"

"Great white sharks!"

"No."

"Electric eels!"

"Nope."

"Stingrays!"

"Not stingrays."

"Giant squid?"

"Nope."

"Mermaids!"

"Those don't exist. Read a book."

"A scuba-diving Sasquatch?"

"Ryan, stop talking."

Finally, our instructor helped us out. "The most dangerous thing in the water, the thing that will most likely kill you or hurt you…" We all slid to the edge of our seats waiting for him to tell us about a crazy mythical creature that devours humans by the dozen. "The most deadly thing in the water is *you*! You are the most dangerous thing in the water. You are the thing that is most likely to hurt you or kill you!"

He then asked us, "What's the most important rule of scuba diving?" We all looked around at one another. I shouted, "Go to the bathroom before you get your wet suit on and hop in the water?" One person laughed awkwardly. One girl wrote it in her notebook.

"The most important rule in scuba diving is that no matter what happens, you *must keep breathing*. Whether you're going up or down, forward or backward, keep breathing."

He then went on to explain that in scuba diving, the pressure is constantly changing. He told us that if we took a breath of air at thirty feet deep and held it in, as we got closer to the surface, it would expand and continue expanding until our lungs burst.

Wow.

This time, I took notes and nobody laughed.

The most important thing you can do while scuba diving is to keep breathing. It keeps you calm and allows the pressure to release and lets you stay alive. Look, I'm not some happy-go-lucky cheerleader who is going to tell you, "Don't worry, be happy," or "Just smile, it will all work out." Sometimes things suck. Sometimes things don't work out the way you want them to. People will bail on you, you will fail at some of the things you try, you will have your heart broken, you will have people tell you you're crazy, that your ideas are stupid, and that the things you want aren't realistic.

You will question yourself and the things you want to do, the places you want to go, the stuff you want to have, and the person you want to be. And then do you know what you are going to do? Like my mom used to tell me when I didn't want to eat my green peas, you are going to plug your nose and eat it. You are going to keep breathing, then move forward.

I hate obstacles almost as much as anybody else not running an actual obstacle course does, but I understand that sometimes stuff happens. All you can do is deal with it and move on.

When you face problems and obstacles as you work toward the things you want to have and do, the places you want to go, and the person you want to be, the most important thing you can do is keep breathing. Just like in scuba diving, if you try to hold those problems in and move forward, they can expand and get bigger, which can result in bigger problems.

Inhale.

Exhale.

Keep breathing.

Every person in history who has worked to get what they want had many moments like these: moments when people said no; moments where they doubted if they could do it; moments of stress, anxiety, and failure.

Let me repeat: you are not alone. It's perfectly normal and OK to run into obstacles, setbacks, and roadblocks. It's OK to feel stress and to doubt yourself from time to time.

There's something else you need to know: *it's perfectly normal and OK to fail*. It happens to everybody all of the time. Everybody you look at and admire has failed a million times. I promise. But the failure didn't define them, and it won't define you. Learn from failure, and keep moving.

WHETHER YOU'RE GOING UP OR DOWN, FORWARD OR BACKWARD, KEEP BREATHING.

There are three things that help me a lot when I run into obstacles or have feelings of self-doubt or need to recalibrate after a failure:

1. **Exercise.** Exercise is a great method of clearing your mind and energizing you to creatively navigate your way around obstacles. It's one of the reasons I'm at the gym just about every day at 6:30 a.m.

   For you, it might not be the gym but getting outside or doing yoga or walking your dog. Whatever it is, staying active and healthy can help you clear your mind, reenergize, reevaluate, and move on.

2. **Start and finish.** Sometimes when you are working on a hard problem that you can't seem to get around or something that is holding you back, just press pause on it and focus on something that has *nothing* to do with the roadblock you're trying to get past. For me, when I'm staring at one of those roadblocks, sometimes I'll stop what I'm doing and clean my house, other times I'll edit a series of photos for Facebook, and other times I'll build something.

   The point is to start and finish something in a short period of time. Completing something will give you confidence, energy, and a revitalized ability to solve difficult problems.

3. **Talk to somebody.** How many times have you had a problem or something holding you back and you kept quiet about it? I know I do this all the time.

   The crazy part is, I also know that as soon as I talk to somebody about it (not necessarily looking for or asking for advice), my mind seems a bit clearer. Talking the problem out with somebody you trust is an awesome way to release stress and see the problem from an angle you might not have considered before.

I urge you that if you have something holding you back or something in your way or feelings of doubt, talk to somebody. If you have nobody to talk to and you feel comfortable with it, talk to a teacher who you trust or ask if they know anybody you can talk to. I promise you that, as weird as it seems or as uncomfortable as it may be at first, there are people around you who want to help. I promise.

Sometimes you have plans, but as things unfold, as obstacles appear, your perfect vision gets blurred, you start to have self-doubt, and all of a sudden, that perfect plan doesn't taste so good. Sometimes you don't even expect those roadblocks. You follow the recipe exactly as you should, you throw it in the oven for the right time at the right temperature, but for some reason, when you take it out and take a bite, it tastes nasty.

Sometimes you make a plan and follow it exactly as you think you should. You have the support of others. You have everything in place and feel confident, but when you move forward, you fail, you run into obstacles, or you get lost.

This doesn't mean that something's wrong with you or your plan—sometimes it's just the way it goes, and many times those obstacles and failures are out of your control. That's OK. But the way you respond to those things and whether or not you let them completely ruin your plan is up to you and your decisions. You *do* have control of what you do after you hit those roadblocks and what you learn from them.

As you set out to make your own lunch, you will undoubtedly run into a few obstacles, things that slow you down. Even though you do everything the way you feel is right, there are bound to be times where things just don't taste good. All you can do is deal with those things the best way you know how to at the time and keep moving forward. Whatever the obstacle is, you're bigger than it. Trust me.

Sometimes the only thing we can do is take a deep breath and keep eating. Isn't that how you're able to eat your aunt's meatloaf with a smile on your face?

Plug Your Nose and Eat It

Of course, it never hurts to make sure you have people around you who you can talk to and to have healthy things to do when you get frustrated or stuck.

When I get caught up in something, I have great friends I can talk to. Sometimes, if it's something really personal, I talk with my family, or if I don't want to tell them, I go for a run, take my dog for a walk, go for a swim, listen to some positive music, or look through old pictures.

Whatever it is, I find something to do to take my mind off the thing that is keeping me down. I clear my head and then revisit the problem after I've released some of that pressure. But I find that the best way to move past the obstacles is to remind myself of the things I'm working toward. I keep files for my goals and dreams, and when I read the stuff I've written, I know that it's all worth it.

If you don't have releases, things to do when you start feeling stressed or frustrated, you can start to go crazy. You might get anxiety attacks or develop health problems. Some people even let their problems push them to using drugs or abusing alcohol, which, of course, is never a good decision. Never.

Whether you're going up or down, forward or backward, keep breathing.

EVEN THOUGH YOU DO EVERYTHING THE WAY YOU FEEL IS RIGHT, THERE ARE BOUND TO BE TIMES WHERE THINGS JUST DON'T TASTE GOOD. ALL YOU CAN DO IS DEAL WITH THOSE THINGS THE BEST WAY YOU KNOW HOW TO AT THE TIME AND KEEP MOVING FORWARD. WHATEVER THE OBSTACLE IS, YOU'RE BIGGER THAN IT. TRUST ME.

MAKE SURE YOU HAVE PEOPLE AROUND YOU WHO YOU CAN TALK TO AND HAVE HEALTHY THINGS TO DO WHEN YOU GET FRUSTRATED OR STUCK.

Side Dish: Sweet & Sour

Choose to See the Good in Every Situation

When life gives you lemons, make orange juice and then wonder how you did it.—Unknown

Two of my favorite people in history were brothers with an extraordinary dream. They had really unfortunate names (Orville and Wilbur), but they had an incredible dream. Have you figured it out yet? They were the same Wright brothers who are usually given credit for flying an aircraft for the first time. Yes, the ones we *just* talked about in the previous chapter.

On the morning of December 17, 1903, these brothers decided to give their flying machine a test run. They called the local newspapers ahead of time so that everyone could read of their awesome feat of flight. Only one newspaper bothered to cover the story, and it was probably because they knew a story about the two crazy dudes in town crashing while trying to fly like birds would sell loads of newspapers.

After a coin toss to decide who would pilot the first attempt, Orville jumped in the seat of the machine. He fired up the engine, and after a brief moment, he started off down the track they had made to help launch the plane into the sky. As the plane headed down the track, I'm sure onlookers were expecting the worst and waiting for the coolest crash they'd ever see.

At this point in history, there was no YouTube where people could watch epic-fail videos. The only time you could watch an epic fail was if you happened to be lucky enough to catch it live!

The plane didn't crash when it reached the end of the track. Instead, a miracle happened. The plane reached the end of the track and left the ground. Orville was flying! To everyone's disbelief, the flyer was actually using an engine to fly. Can you imagine the excitement? Can you imagine what it looked like? Nobody had ever been off the ground like that before in history!

Orville hardly had time to be excited, because after twelve seconds in the air, the plane fell back to the ground, smashing the rudder and breaking a lever off the engine. Orville had only managed to travel a distance of 120 feet. Fail.

Fail?

They had twelve seconds in the sky, 120 feet, and a broken airplane to their names. I'm sure the spectators were brutally disappointed. Some may have even laughed at the weak attempt at flight. I am sure one guy even wanted to text his friend and tell him, but because there were no cell phones, he had to send a carrier pigeon and wait three days to get a response.

The crowd chalked it up as another failure for these two brothers. A bunch of people must have concluded that the brothers were legitimately crazy and that engine-powered flight was impossible. Do you know what the brothers did? They celebrated, because they were ecstatic that they had managed to fly twelve seconds and a distance of 120 feet. They knew they were that much closer to flying higher, longer, and greater distances! After a quick repair, Wilbur jumped in the airplane and had a try at flying the craft.

Their final attempt for the day produced a fifty-nine-second flight covering 852 feet! It gives me goose bumps thinking about it. These brothers had a vision. There were a ton of people who told them it was crazy, a bunch of folks who tried to stop them from achieving their dream of flight, and a million others who thought it would never happen. The brothers, however, never let go of their vision, their dream, and their goal. The Wright brothers changed history because of their persistence and vision.

You have things you dream about and have a vision for your future. Do you give in and give up the first time something doesn't work out? Do you listen to the crowd when they tell you you're crazy? Do you let your friends, family, and strangers shoot you down every time they tell you something's not realistic? Are you focused on your vision? Are you celebrating your small victories along the way? Your twelve seconds and 120 feet in the air?

It's easy to be overwhelmed and weighed-down by a vision for bigger, better, and more, but it's so important to take time to look at what you've already done and see the signs that you're that much closer to your goal. You've made it through a bunch of different grades of school. You have passed tests. Maybe you've got your first part-time job or driver's license. Maybe you spent last summer building houses for a charity or volunteered with kids in your community. Perhaps you're on your school's student council or sports teams. There are a million different things for you to celebrate.

Without a doubt, there will be times when you will crash after barely leaving the ground, leaving your plane in need of repair, but celebrate the fact that you actually left the ground. Never release your vision, your dream, or your goal. When things don't go as planned, it's up to you to decide to see sweet when everybody else sees sour.

20

SPIT IT OUT

How to quit the stuff that's holding you back and politely reject the naysayers you love who love you too.

WHAT DO JAY-Z, KANYE WEST, THE MRS. FIELDS COOKIE LADY, BILL GATES, WALT DISNEY, RICHARD BRANSON, CHRISTINA AGUILERA, STEVE JOBS, TED TURNER, MARK TWAIN, AND MARK ZUCKERBERG ALL HAVE IN COMMON? EVERY ONE OF THEM MADE YOUR GRANDMA VERY, VERY ANGRY BY DEBUNKING HER INSIGHT THAT QUITTERS NEVER WIN.

I have a rap beef with the grandmothers of this earth. There's a slight possibility I might get in the booth and record a dis record and call them out for all of their shenanigans. It will feature 50 Cent and Eminem, and it will be an instant hip-hop classic. But until I can lay down my verse, I have a message for grandmothers:

Dear sweet, sweet little old grandmas around the planet: You. Are. Wrong!

Don't get me wrong. You are still the nicest people on this planet. Your ancient remedies cure the harshest colds, horrifying night terrors, itchy mosquito bites, and aching broken hearts.

Your gingersnaps are still delicious golden treats delivered from the cookie gods wrapped in baby dreams, and your sweet tea is like liquid rainbows in a glass, sweetened by powdered unicorn horn. But you were wrong once.

You weren't wrong about not talking to strangers or saving my pennies. You weren't wrong about always saying please and thank you or holding the door for girls.

But you were totally, utterly, and ridiculously wrong when you told me and other children around the world, "winners never quit."

Here's a newsflash for the grannies of the globe: winners quit all the time. In fact, winners quit just about everything. They quit everything that isn't related to the things they want to have, the places they want to go, the stuff they want to do, and the person they want to be.

They quit toxic relationships. They quit colleges that aren't bringing them closer to the career they want. They quit jobs they hate. They quit everything that doesn't have *anything* to do with the life they want.

I'm going to break it down for you like this: if there is something you don't want to do and it has nothing to do with the life you want, *quit*!

I've seen too many students go through four years of college in programs they aren't interested in, at schools they hate, just because they were afraid of quitting. I have friends who wake up every day hating their jobs and the people they work with, but they are too afraid to quit, because, of course, winners never quit.

See what you've done, Grandma? I hope you're happy.

To get the stuff you want, you need to quit the stuff you don't want. Sometimes this means saying good-bye to friends or leaving places you're comfortable in. Other times it might mean disappointing the people who love you. But those people don't have to wake up in your skin every day and feel confident looking in the mirror and saying, "I am happy."

I'm a huge fan of hip-hop and have been a fan of Kanye West since before he started releasing his own albums. So there. I remember how excited I was when I heard he would be releasing his first album, *The College Dropout*.

I bought the album the day it came out and listened to the whole thing as soon as I got home. I remember thinking how interesting it was that his album had a bunch of stories about his decision to quit college to pursue music full time. He knew music was what he wanted to be doing, and he believed his college education was interfering with his dreams and music goals, so he dropped everything and focused only on music.

What are two or three things you could quit right now to allow yourself more time, energy, and opportunities to focus on the things you really want?

Quit playing Xbox if you want to get better at playing the guitar. Quit those unhealthy habits if you want to get in shape and feel better. Quit listening to angry or depressing music if you want to feel happier. Quit wasting your time online if you want to have more confidence around people.

I do have one rule, however. Quitting high school is not an option. Anything else is fair game, but high school is one of those things that you are better off finishing before making decisions about your next steps.

History is made by quitters. Bill Gates quit Harvard to make computers. Mark Zuckerberg left college to work on Facebook. Jay-Z quit selling drugs to start recording music. Your dude Ben Affleck quit college *twice* to become an actor. Everyone's favorite billionaire and founder of Virgin Records, Virgin Airlines, and Virgin Galactic, Richard Branson, quit high school when he was sixteen years old.

TO GET THE STUFF YOU WANT, YOU NEED TO QUIT THE STUFF YOU DON'T WANT. SOMETIMES THIS MEANS SAYING GOOD-BYE TO FRIENDS OR LEAVING PLACES YOU'RE COMFORTABLE IN.

I MADE MY OWN LUNCH

SOOZIE

Soozie grew up on a mountain—literally. She was always encouraged to be creative while she was growing up. Her creativity, ingenuity, and enthusiasm for life were always being celebrated. But when it came time to make decisions about college, her family's finances made the decision pretty clear—going to college was not possible.

Soozie began looking at possible career paths. She tried retail, restaurants, child care, and a wide array of others. She always did well, was praised by her bosses, made great money, and was even given management opportunities. But none of those paths or opportunities scratched her creativity that was once celebrated.

Soozie was working at a bank and moving up the ranks fast. The constant positive feedback from customers, coworkers, and bosses eventually had her promoted from a bank teller to a loan officer.

One day, Soozie had a client come in who was planning a wedding and happened to mention to Soozie that she couldn't find a photographer. Remembering the fun she had had as a photographer's assistant in high school, Soozie jumped at the chance to offer her services as a photographer.

Although she didn't "quit her day job" that day, Soozie took that chance to change her career path. Soon after, she quit her job and began pursuing her passion for photography and turned her creative outlet into her dream career.

Soozie started her own business, and she is now a highly sought-after photographer for a ton of different types of events. Check out her work at www .photographybysoozie.com.

Soozie's decision to quit her job at the bank allowed her to find a career that she absolutely loves.

The bottom line is simple: if it's something that is not at all related to the things you want, quit it and start spending more time on the things you do want. Just make sure the things you're quitting aren't affecting the other stuff you want. For example, if you want to take a three-month trip to Nicaragua but decide you hate your job at the mall and that you've had enough, make sure you have something else lined up to help pay for your adventure.

IF IT'S SOMETHING THAT IS NOT AT ALL RELATED TO THE THINGS YOU WANT, QUIT IT AND START SPENDING MORE TIME ON THE THINGS YOU DO WANT.

A famous rapper from the 1990s wrote a song called "2 Legit 2 Quit." He couldn't have been more wrong. Winners quit. They quit anything that is interfering with their vision of the stuff they want to have, the places they want to go, the things they want to do, and the person they want to become. Thanks for nothing, MC Hammer. I'm now beefing with you *and* your grandma.

It's now time for me to hit the recording booth.

It's OK to Burp—Just Say Excuse Me

Sometimes doing what you want means saying no to the people who care about you. Never, ever apologize for living your life the way you want. But sometimes you might need to say sorry if doing what you want means upsetting the people around you.

→ My youngest brother, Dallin, and I climbed into a nine-seater van with fifteen fellow backpackers and two Guatemalan drivers. We left our bridge, caves, and hostel in Semuc Champey to travel to the far north of Guatemala to discover some ancient Mayan temple ruins.

Well, to be honest, we weren't going to be the first to discover the ruins. They were discovered a long time ago, and we were going just to look at them. But that sounds boring, so I used the word *discover*.

After about four hours of driving through the Guatemalan mountains without seeing anything but trees, clouds, and the back of our driver's head, we hit a traffic jam. I didn't get it. There was only one road. We were in the middle of nowhere. How was this possible?

The driver got out of the van and went to speak to some of the people ahead of us. He came back and said something to us in Spanish, which I don't speak. I know for sure he didn't say, "You aren't in Kansas anymore." I would've been relieved if we *had* been in Kansas, because the last time I was there was a few months earlier for work, and they spoke English.

Our driver pulled out onto the wrong side of the road, completely clear of traffic, and we began to pass all of the stopped vehicles. Anytime somebody stopped us for passing the backed-up traffic, our driver or his sidekick would shout, "*Turismo!*" We passed hundreds of other vehicles, maybe even more than a thousand, and then came to a quick stop behind a few other vans that looked like ours and were filled with people who looked like us.

Our driver and his buddy got out of our van and went to get some more information as the fifteen backpackers in our van piled out to meet the backpackers in the other vans. After speaking with them, we learned that there was a huge protest going on up ahead and that the protesters had been blocking traffic for two days and weren't planning on letting anybody through. Now, this isn't exactly like the protest you had last week in your town to stop them from cutting down the town's oldest maple tree. This was a protest in which the people protesting blocked off a section of the only road connecting major cities and protected the line with machetes and even a few shotguns and an AK-47 or two.

We walked ahead to scout out the protest and to figure out what we were going to do now that we were stopped in the middle-of-nowhere Guatemala. We approached the line and saw people holding banners and signs. Others were shouting things in Spanish; some were resting in the shade, but all of them were looking at us.

Dallin asked, "What are we going to do?"

"Follow me."

We walked back to our *turismo* van and got our backpacks, then went to talk with the other backpackers. We started explaining the situation. "Look, if we are here on this side going that way, there has to be another group of backpackers just like us on the other side coming this way. All we have to do is cross the pro-test line and get in their *turismo* vans and send them to get in ours."

A few of the backpackers looked really nervous as we approached the protest line. As we got to the protest line, I looked at Dallin and said, "Let's do this." Dallin and I led the way, followed by about forty other backpackers. Every one of us crossed the line with our backpacks on. The shouting became a lot louder as I looked back and saw a few of the men shaking their machetes in the air toward us. Dallin must've seen them too, because he looked at me and asked, "What are we supposed to do?"

I snapped a picture. "Keep walking."

When we got to the other side, one of the girls in our group who spoke and understood Spanish came running up and said, "Didn't you hear those guys shouting? They were *not* happy that you crossed their line."

I figured as much.

A group of protestors was starting to gather around us, some curious, some furious. I asked our Spanish-speaking backpacker friend if she could do me a favor.

"Could you please explain our situation to these protestors? We just want to get across to continue traveling in their beautiful country. We had no intention of offending them, and we are sorry for trekking through their protest." She broke away from our group, and I watched her speak to one of the men. The conversation finished with a smile, a *gracias*, and a handshake.

You constantly have people around you protesting, objecting to things you do or do not do, things they want you to do instead.

Your parents protest against your decision to leave home and go backpacking through Europe for a year. Your friends protest against your decision to stay home this weekend to study.

Your guidance counselor insists that you listen to her advice and go to the university that she thinks is best.

Your boyfriend or girlfriend protests against your dream of becoming a photographer.

Sometimes you have to go against their protests. Sometimes you have to ignore their objections and apologize when you get to the other side.

Now when I say apologize, I am by no means suggesting that you apologize for living the way you want. Never apologize for carving your own path. Don't ever say sorry for doing the things you are passionate about.

However, along the way, you are bound to upset people close to you, people who love you and care about you, people who may have had different plans for you. Say sorry for upsetting them or going against the plans they had and continue along your path. At the end of the day, they want to see you happy, and that's what this is about. They will get it soon enough.

It's OK to say no to your parents.

It's OK to go against plans your friends have for your life.

It's fine to choose something other than the options your guidance counselor presents.

It's not bad to say no to your boyfriend or girlfriend.

NEVER APOLOGIZE FOR CARVING YOUR OWN PATH. DON'T EVER SAY SORRY FOR DOING THE THINGS YOU ARE PASSIONATE ABOUT.

Of course, they will get mad. They might cry. They may mention you in a Facebook update or even write a blog post about you. It's OK. This isn't a green light for you to be rude or disrespectful, but sometimes you have to cross protest lines to get closer to where you're going.

So your parents are pressuring you to give up your European trip to go to college in the fall, but you don't want to. They're not doing it simply because they want to upset you or start a huge fight. It's because they care and they want to keep you safe.

If you're serious about that trip to Europe, bring them a plan. Show them how you plan to save money from your job to pay for it. Not something that just says, "I'll save money." Give them details. How much money will you save? How often? Show them the places you want to go and what you want to do. Show them that you've researched the prices of travel insurance. Bring them evidence of other people who have successfully done something similar. Show them blogs, pictures, and videos of people in the places you want to go.

Go even further. Give them an action plan on how you'll be ready to pursue college when you get back. Show them that you know all about the application process, deadlines, and requirements. You can even show them that a European trip will add a ton of insight and experience for your admissions essay.

Let them know how serious you are, politely ask for their support, and explain what it will mean to have that support.

And if they still protest? Go anyway (as long as it's legal and you'll still have a home to come back to) and apologize for hurting or disobeying them.

Your boyfriend keeps telling you that you should give up your dream of becoming a photographer because it isn't *realistic*. Tell him *why* you want to do it and how you feel. Tell him the plan you've made. Show him people who have taken a similar route and how they are doing now. Find a mentor and somewhere to volunteer to show how serious you are about it. If he still protests, do it anyway and apologize for not taking his advice. Remember, you aren't sorry for living your dreams. You are sorry that you may have upset him.

It's hard for your parents, teachers, and friends to see you going against their advice, but in most cases, if you are honest with them and tell them why, show them examples of others who have done something similar before you, give them the details of your plan, and genuinely ask for their support, then they will start to understand.

You know what you want. You've decided what you will have, where you will go, what you will do, and who you will be. Now it's time for you to get it. In your quest to make your own lunch, you are bound to upset some people along the way, and it's OK. Keep moving forward.

It's OK to burp sometimes; just don't be rude about it. Say, "Excuse me."

YOU KNOW WHAT YOU WANT. YOU'VE DECIDED WHAT YOU WILL HAVE, WHERE YOU WILL GO, WHAT YOU WILL DO, AND WHO YOU WILL BE. NOW IT'S TIME FOR YOU TO GET IT.

STEP 5

CHOCOLATE-COVERED EVERYTHING: REAP THE REWARDS OF HARD WORK, REALIZED DREAMS, AND ALL THINGS SWEET

21

YOUR FOOD IS GETTING COLD

Procrastination is not a Recommended Daily Intake.

Start doing something with your epic ideas now!

STOP WAITING FOR THE RIGHT TIME! IT DOESN'T EXIST. THE RIGHT TIME IS THE TIME THAT YOU DECIDE TO ACTUALLY DO SOMETHING. #WISDOM

It's pretty much a fact (and by fact I mean I just made this up right now) that there are only three groups of people in this world when it comes to how they spend their time.

Group number one we need to thank. Group number one is responsible for all of the fail videos on YouTube. Group number one spends their time thinking very little and doing a whole lot. In fact, the science (and by science I mean the numbers I just made up in my head) says that this group spends 3 percent of their time thinking and 97 percent of their time doing. Not the best ratio.

And do you want to know how to tell if somebody from this group has just used their 3 percent thinking? Their next sentence will always start with these words: "I've got an idea." Yup. Every fail video on YouTube started with those very words.

Group two is very different from group one. Group two spends 100 percent of their time talking. They talk about what's wrong with the world, what's wrong with their school, what's wrong with their friends, and what's wrong with my Canadian accent.

They spend all of their time talking and none of their time doing.

Group three, you ask? They're the ones who have it figured out. They spend an equal amount of their time thinking, talking, and doing.

They think about changes they could make, they talk with people about those things, and then they do them. And because they've thought about it and talked it out, their decisions end up being great decisions.

The people in group three are the ones who make our schools, communities, and our world a better place.

Unfortunately for me, in high school, I was a strong candidate for captain of group one.

→ I remember one day in high school, I had the day off school and got together with two of my friends.

We were sitting around in my friend's basement when the conversation started the exact same way every other epic conversation in history has started.

"What do you wanna do?" My friend cleverly responded, "I dunno. What do you wanna do?" My other friend added his opinion. "No idea. What do you wanna do?" I finally answered. "Whatever, dude. What do you wanna do?" Clearly, we were very sophisticated specimens.

A huge smile took over my friend's face as he delivered the details of the 3 percent thinking he had just used. He spoke slowly and clearly to make sure we didn't get lost in the complicated details. "Let's drive around in the Ratmobile and throw firecrackers out of the window!"

Awesome.

(MTV-style warning: Please, please, please do not attempt to do this ever…and I mean ever. And if you do, please don't send me the YouTube link. I do not want to be an accessory to your crimes.)

The three of us jumped off the sofa, grabbed the bag of firecrackers my friend had bought on a recent hockey road trip to Florida, and ran to the car.

We started driving around my parents' neighborhood while my friend began lighting firecrackers and throwing them out the window.

Here's a quick little math and science lesson: I was driving about twenty-five miles an hour. The wick of the firecracker took about ten seconds to burn down, so by the time the firecracker was lit, thrown out the window, and I kept driving, it was, like, a hundred yards behind us when it exploded.

We could barely hear the bang.

Then a miracle happened.

By some freak of nature and glitch in the space-time continuum, my friend—the same genius who came up with the first idea—was granted another 3 percent of thinking. "Dude…I've got a better idea…" His eyes lit up as he thought it over for a second time, still barely able to believe he came up with it. "I'm going to light the firecracker…" He raised his voice as we moved in closer. "*And hold on to it longer!*"

High fives for everybody.

"That's an awesome idea!"

My friend took a firecracker out of the bag, looked at me through the rear-view mirror as I continued to drive, and then, with a look of accomplishment on his face like he just deciphered a World War II enemy code using Pop Tarts and toothpicks, he lit the firecracker in his hand.

The next ten seconds went as follows.

I looked up at my rearview mirror to check on him and then back down at the road. Up at the mirror, down to the road. Up at the mirror, back to the road. Up to the mirror once more—and that's when I saw it. A police car. It turned right behind us, going in the same direction. There were maybe forty yards separating our vehicle of criminal offenses and their vehicle of Taser power and rubber bullets.

There was no way I could stay cool. "Yo. Cops!"

He looked at me. He looked at the ground. He looked at the burning firecracker. He looked at the window. He panicked.

I saw a road on my right-hand side. I put my turn signal on and began to turn down the road as I looked one more time into my rearview mirror.

I saw my friend's face, taken over with a look of shame, guilt, and failure.

As I watched him in the mirror, I saw him drop his head in defeat. He then did something that I still struggle to comprehend. I saw him lift one leg and place the burning firecracker under his butt.

I turned the corner, and the police car passed by, then I heard it.

Bang!

An explosion, followed by a giant yelp.

What an idiot!

He *literally* missed his window of opportunity by holding on to the firecracker for so long. And by holding on to it that long, he caused himself a bunch of pain that he didn't necessarily need or want!

How often do *you* do that? I'm not talking about sitting on *actual* firecrackers. What I mean is how often do you hold on to your ideas too long, waiting for the right time? How often do you tell yourself, *Just a little bit longer*?

Sound familiar?

There are going to be times where you have great ideas. You're going to think of people to talk to and things to do. You're going to have ideas of places to visit, jobs to apply for, and organizations to volunteer with. And if you're like most people, you're going to find yourself waiting. Waiting for the right time, waiting until you have more money, waiting until you're older, waiting until you finish college, waiting until you're married, waiting until you have kids, waiting until the kids grow up—waiting, waiting, waiting.

Forget all that stuff and do it! Have the things you want to have, go to the places you want to go, do the stuff you want to do, and be the person you want to be.

You have the chance to do whatever you want *right now*. There are way too many people sitting around holding on to their amazing ideas who end up waiting way too long. Then one day twenty years down the road, when they are thirty-seven with three kids and two mortgages, they look back and say, "I shouldn't have waited."

YOU HAVE THE CHANCE TO DO WHATEVER YOU WANT *RIGHT NOW*. THERE ARE WAY TOO MANY PEOPLE SITTING AROUND HOLDING ON TO THEIR AMAZING IDEAS WHO END UP WAITING WAY TOO LONG.

I MADE MY OWN LUNCH

JESSE

Growing up, Jesse was always encouraged to do what she loved. Like her mother, who bypassed college to start a dance studio, Jesse loved dancing. And without any real influence to follow a college track, Jesse never included college in her plans.

She taught dance at her mother's studio throughout high school, and although she was making great money for somebody her age, she wasn't really concerned with a career path at the time.

Jesse's aunt surprised her one day by entering her into a modeling contest. The next thing she knew, she had an agent and a modeling career. She was given amazing opportunities for travel and exploration, but she didn't love modeling the way she used to love teaching dance.

Jesse found herself thinking, "What's next?" But before she got too far in her planning to switch careers, she was diagnosed with rheumatoid arthritis.

If anybody had a perfect excuse to wait or sit back and hold out for a better time, it was Jesse. But Jesse decided to go full steam ahead with her plans.

She decided to fight the disease through yoga, diet, and meditation. And while fighting her disease, she found her way back to the beginning (and her first love)—teaching people about their bodies, movement, and harmony as a certified yoga instructor.

In sharing her story, knowledge, ideas, and philosophies, Jesse began healing others as well as herself. And to her surprise, her modeling career took off for a second time…but this time it was on *her* terms.

Jesse found herself on the covers of the *New York Times Magazine* and *Yoga International*, and as the face of Lucy Sport and Under Armour. At this point, she realized that her career and her passion merged on the same path.

She eventually went back to school to be a holistic health practitioner. Now she shares her experience and insights on her blog, *The Golden Secrets* (check out www.thegoldensecrets.org).

Jesse was never sitting in the backseat of a 1987 Plymouth Sundance with a firecracker in her hand, waiting for the right time. She decided that waiting was the worst thing she could've done, and she acted.

Stop waiting. Start acting.

The people you consider successful didn't become successful by waiting for the right time. They *made* the right time by acting. Remember what I wrote a few pages ago? The right time doesn't exist. The right time is the time that you decide to act. I hate to keep saying the same thing over and over, but do you see how powerful your decisions are?

There are things that you can be doing *right now* to help you live the life you want. I promise. Remember your Recommended Daily Intake of action? Break your vision into bite-sized pieces.

Make Your Own Lunch isn't just some cute story about some construction workers. It's not just a book telling stories of some weird, skinny, awkward kid from a small town in Canada. It's about *you*.

Make Your Own Lunch is, as you must know by now, about decision. It's about taking time to learn about yourself and what you really want. It's about understanding your menu and what your options are right now. It's about deciding for yourself what's realistic or not. It's about deciding what you want, making a plan, and cutting that plan into bite-sized pieces.

Make Your Own Lunch is about you taking your ideas about the things you'll have, the places you'll go, the stuff you'll do, and the person you'll be and putting those ideas into action right now, with what you have, to the best of your ability.

By not acting right now, by holding on to those ideas and the things you want to do, you're sitting on a firecracker. And remember what happens to the geniuses who hold on to firecrackers? Exactly.

Don't Skip Lunch

What are you waiting for?

So I want to try a little challenge with you. I want you to stare at the word on the next page for one minute and rearrange the letters to spell new words and write them in the space provided. I want you to see how many words you can get in a minute. Get as many unique words as you can, so the three- and four-letter words might not be enough on this one.

Set a clock or timer, then go.

PROCRASTINATE

Here's where things get really weird. Here's where I guess some of the words you had and get a lot of them right. Here's a list of some of the most impressive and disturbing words that have ever been yelled at me while onstage:

- Rat
- Tin
- Cast
- Pro
- Creation
- Creations
- Aristocrat
- Crap roast (welcome to Illinois)
- Rasta
- Racist
- Prostate
- Spartan
- Pro-star

It's pretty amazing, because this is something I do from stage when I'm speaking all over the continent. I've done this exercise in front of more than five hundred thousand teens across the United States and Canada. I know the words people will shout out, and I have, by now, heard just about every word.

Except one: *castrate*.

Yup.

Chances are that if you're a girl, you are laughing. If you're a guy, you're starting to sweat, and if you're under the age of fourteen, you're confused.

Usually, when I get to this part of my presentation, all of the girls giggle, the dudes wince in pain, and the teachers call security. As I'm being chased off the stage, I put the dictionary definition of the word *castrate* on the screen and somehow that settles everybody down.

The dictionary defines *castrate* like this: "To remove spirit or render ineffective, especially by psychological means." Bet you thought it would be something different. It doesn't say anything about cutting, and there's nothing about pain or guys!

Isn't this *exactly* what you do to yourself when you procrastinate? You render yourself *ineffective*, which means not working. By procrastinating, you're not working. You're ineffective.

I'm not talking about procrastinating handing in an assignment, taking out the trash, studying for a test, or buying a birthday present for your best friend's birthday party. I'm talking about procrastinating making decisions about the things you really want to have, the places you want to go, the stuff you want to try, and the person you dream of becoming. By procrastinating, you're castrating yourself. And this isn't limited to guys.

Procrastinating isn't the same thing as taking time to understand your menu;

procrastinating is lying on your sofa playing *Call of Duty* for the seventeenth straight hour when you could be working to get closer to your dream of becoming a professional motocross rider.

Procrastinating is watching the eleventh episode of any kind of MTV marathon when you could be doing things that bring you closer to the European vacation you've decided to take in the summer with your best friend.

If you find yourself procrastinating, stop it right now. Do something, do *anything*, that takes you away from that thing you are using to procrastinate.

Are you about to start your fourth hour of playing Xbox? Turn the console off and make a list of things that you could be doing instead. Or maybe you don't make a list, maybe you know one or two things that you could be doing right now, so start with those.

Procrastinating is completely normal. Everybody procrastinates at some point or another. But let's be honest with each other. Procrastinating is a lot like peeing your pants. It might be the easier thing to do at the time, but in the long run? Probably not the best decision.

You have the chance right now to take a step closer to the things you want to have. You have a chance to start making a difference in your school and in your community at this very moment.

In your school, there are things you could be doing right now to bring you closer to that stuff you want. Your dream of becoming a photographer? Go and chat with the yearbook committee and ask if they could use some of your shots for the yearbook. The trip to Italy you've decided to take? You could be working at an Italian bakery or taking Italian lessons with your friend's Italian grandmother.

You community has a ton of opportunities as well. There are countless ways to get involved with community events, initiatives, and organizations. Unfortunately, most people would rather sit at home on YouTube than actually working toward the stuff they want.

The good thing is that you aren't most people. You've decided to take action, and you've decided to take those actions today and every day that follows until you are living your epically epic life of epicness.

Stop *castrating* yourself and start being effective.

22

ITADAKIMASU

It's time to say thank you.

As I write this, I'm actually sitting on a train looking out the window at snowcapped Mount Fuji on my way to Tokyo's Narita Airport. I'm in Japan—*again*!

You're probably sick of hearing that by now, but I love being here. There's something I feel every time I come to Japan that reminds me of how much control we have over the adventures we set out on and the things we learn. I decided to shoot out here for a few weeks to rejuvenate and visit some places I've never been to before. There are so many things I love about Japan, none of which is dressing up like anime characters and reenacting fight scenes from my favorite animated movies and video games.

The stuff I love most about Japan is the little cultural differences. Stuff like using more respectful words when speaking to people older than you or welcoming spring by throwing soybeans in your house. Honestly, tell me your house couldn't use some soybeans being thrown in it? That's what I thought.

There's something else I love about Japan, and it's something that happens every time you sit down to eat. In Japan, before you eat a meal, when everyone is seated and getting ready to dig in, it's customary to say, *"Itadakimasu!"* (ee-tah-dah-kee-mass). There is no literal translation to English, but it basically means "thank you for this meal I am about to receive." It has nothing to do with religion. It's just to show thanks.

I wonder why more people don't do this in other cultures, and not just before eating, but for everything they have and everything they are planning to have.

You have amazing things waiting for you. You have epic adventures around the corner, incredible friends to be made, people waiting for you to make a difference in their lives, jobs to be worked, unforgettable experiences to be experienced, and awesome places to go. It's time to say thanks for the stuff you have and the stuff you are getting ready to receive, because the best way to get more of the stuff you want is to be thankful for the things you have.

It kind of works like this: have you ever seen a pair of shoes or haircut or T-shirt you really wanted? You walk into the mall or see something on TV that you decide you *need* to get. The next day at school you see somebody wearing the exact same shirt you want. Later in the day, while you're ordering your vanilla latte at Starbucks, the cashier is rocking the same haircut you decided you want. Your best friend's brother has the shoes you want, and that random person in the car beside you at the red light is eating the exact same thing you wanted for dinner.

Has this happened to you before?

It's because when you decide that you want something, you turn your brain into a police search dog. You know the ones? They just need a single sniff of what they're looking for and they're able to track it down.

Once you tell your brain what to look for—what you are thankful for—it starts doing whatever it can to find it. That's why you start seeing that stuff that you want all over the place. The same thing goes for being thankful for the things you have.

Once you realize that you appreciate a certain thing, your brain races to find more of it so that you can continue to be thankful. I don't care who you are or what has happened to you in your life; you have countless things to be thankful for.

If you're able to feel thanks for those things, things that you have or things you are getting ready to have, your brain goes out looking for them. It knows you like them, and they make you feel great, so your brain wants to bring it to you.

What are you thankful for? Health? Your boyfriend or girlfriend? Family? Friends? Teachers? Facebook? Netflix? *Angry Birds*? Your grandma's blueberry muffins? I'm sure there are a ton of things that you are thankful for.

Even if you feel that there's nothing you're thankful for right now, there are things that you know you will have, places you know you will go, stuff you know you will do, and the person you know you will become, so start there. Be thankful for that because that stuff is on its way. You've decided so.

You've decided to get what you want and are willing to cut off every other option. It's time to give a little bow and say *itadakimasu*. Thank you for this epic life I am getting ready to receive.

IT'S TIME TO SAY THANKS
FOR THE STUFF YOU HAVE
AND THE STUFF YOU ARE
GETTING READY TO RECEIVE,
BECAUSE THE BEST WAY TO
GET MORE OF THE STUFF YOU
WANT IS TO BE THANKFUL
FOR THE THINGS YOU HAVE.

23

DIG IN

Begin living your epically epic life of work, travel, wonder, and (maybe) college.

So, here we are, at the end of this book. It's kind of like the end of a first date, but without the awkward head butt as you move in for the first kiss (always go right).

During the course of this book:

You may have laughed at the stupidity of Bob and his peanut butter sandwiches.

You read my adventures in Japan—the raw horse, the *shirako*, and the kimono incident.

You read about my friend Leila, who is living her dream life traveling the globe and being a writer.

You learned about Paul, who was questioning what he should do with his life and ended up starting a nonprofit organization to get skateboards to kids around the world who can't afford them.

You may have been inspired by the legacy of Terry Fox, the young Canadian who, in his early twenties, decided to run across Canada to raise money for cancer research and died during his quest, leaving behind a legacy of courage, sacrifice, and bravery.

You found out that I have a rap beef with your grandma. Look for the dis record to hit the radio in the next few months.

You saw from the story of the Wright brothers the importance of getting excited about what others assume are failures.

You heard about my travels to Guatemala, Slovakia, Honduras, and more, and may have started dreaming about the places you will go.

So now what?

Now, you start…Now you dig in.

While you were reading this book, you made some decisions. You've decided some of the things you want to have, you've decided where you're going, you've made decisions about what you'll do, and you've decided the type of person you'll be.

It's time to start having those things, going to those places, doing that stuff, and becoming that person.

I know you might be thinking, *Ryan, this all sounds nice, but let's be honest…I'm supposed to be getting ready for college. I can't be wasting my time daydreaming about giving shoes to poor children in Uruguay, taking African safaris, and riding in tuk-tuks in Thailand.*

Wrong. That's exactly what you *must* do if that's what your dream is. Start seeing those things, decide they are realistic, and start doing them. College, if it's right for you, will always be there after you've started laying out the things you *must* do. There's no rule that you *have* to go to college if it's not your path. As you saw in this book, there are a ton of people living epic lives without college. Don't believe me? Check out www.raiseyourflag.com.

If you have a school that you are dreaming about going to, what are you waiting for? Start figuring out now what it will take to get there and start working toward that.

Too many people tell themselves that the stuff they want is not possible. They put their decisions on the back burner, or even worse, they decide they're not realistic. They tell themselves they can't do it, they don't have time, or that they don't deserve it, and they settle. They settle for crappy jobs. They settle for a major that they hate. They settle for a boyfriend or girlfriend who makes them feel like garbage, and they settle in every other area of their lives.

You have the chance right now to decide not to settle. To *never* settle.

Decide that you will have all the things you want. If people tell you it's not realistic or that you can't do it, don't listen. Block them out and instead focus so much on the stuff you want that you can taste it.

Do it, because if you don't, no one else will do it for you. Do it because you know you can. Do it because others think you can't. Do it because you won't be happy if you don't. Whatever the reason, just do it.

Making your own lunch will sometimes involve cutting off friends who are holding you back. It might mean upsetting your parents when you tell them that you don't want to become a pharmacist and that your dream is to teach guitar lessons in Poland.

DECIDE THAT YOU WILL HAVE ALL THE THINGS YOU WANT. IF PEOPLE TELL YOU IT'S NOT REALISTIC OR THAT YOU CAN'T DO IT, DON'T LISTEN. BLOCK THEM OUT AND INSTEAD FOCUS SO MUCH ON THE STUFF YOU WANT THAT YOU CAN TASTE IT.

Sometimes it will seem easier than using the Magic Bullet to make three-second smoothies, and at other times harder than beating my mom in an arm wrestle. (Which, for the record has only been done once…by Bigfoot. My mom was using her left hand while knitting a cardigan with her right.)

Sometimes, you will find yourself wondering if it's worth it. I can guarantee you that it is. It is *so* worth it.

By reading this book, you've been given a handful of burning firecrackers. Those firecrackers are your ideas, your inspiration, your decisions, your feelings, and your plan.

You get to decide what you will do with them. Will you start now? Or will you sit on them and wait for the right time?

Will you sit at the top of the skyscraper you're building and complain about the peanut butter sandwich in your lunch box, or will you *make your own lunch*?

There are tons of people out there living the exact lives they want to be living— teachers, parents, artists, Zamboni drivers, rock stars, athletes, park rangers, window washers, bike couriers, doctors, disposable camera repair people, and music producers.

There are so many people who are waking up every day living the life of their dreams. Why shouldn't you be one of them?

So…it's time. It's time to throw the peanut butter sandwich down, ditch the lunch box, and have what you want.

It's time to put this book down. It's time to decide that you will have exactly what you want, go exactly where you want to go, do exactly what you want to do, and be exactly who you want to be. You'll know when to stay where you are and when to move on to another adventure.

You *never* need to answer the question, "What do you want to be when you grow up?" You can spend your time answering other questions and having the time of your life.

You will have awesome experiences. You will wander. You will wonder. You will travel. You might go to college. You will live an epic life.

How do I know? Because you make your own lunch.

IT'S TIME TO PUT THIS BOOK DOWN. IT'S TIME TO DECIDE THAT YOU WILL HAVE EXACTLY WHAT YOU WANT, GO EXACTLY WHERE YOU WANT TO GO, DO EXACTLY WHAT YOU WANT TO DO, AND BE EXACTLY WHO YOU WANT TO BE.

BIG-UPS & SHOUT-OUTS

Contrary to popular belief, I was not raised by a family of elephant seals on a glacier in the Canadian Arctic. There have been a lot of people involved in me making my own lunch. The following people are just a few of the people who helped me, taught me, laughed at me, laughed with me, and kept me out of prison:

Seiko: It's called love. For saying yes when I got down on one knee in front of all of those strangers in Shinjuku. For always understanding. For laughing with me and at me. For loving me, supporting me, and sharing your life with me.

Mom and Dad: Thank you for always supporting me and my crazy ideas and adventures, and thanks for just being awesome parents. I know it wasn't easy raising the five of us. I love you both.

Dan: For teaching me how to get into trouble and talk my way out of it. Also, for *always* being later than me.

Jacqueline: For showing me that writing can be funny, even if it's never, ever fun. Ever.

Jonathan: For waiting until I make a funny joke and then hijacking it by making it funnier.

Dallin: For not being a baby, even though you are the baby. Also, who put scissors in the baby's pocket?!

Auntie Gayle: For being my second mom when my actual mom forgot me at the mall, school, or airport.

Matt: I've looked up to you for as long as I can remember. Literally. You're six foot five and three-quarters. I have to look up to you.

Kelly: I'll explain the jokes to you after. Thanks for always laughing at our ridiculous family stories.

Tom P: You've reached dad joke level 10. Congratulations. Thank you for supporting this *Make Your Own Lunch* thing since you first heard of it.

Granddad: For being the greatest storyteller of all time.

Big Phil: Thanks for being a bro, my memory, my workout buddy, and my personal security. You won't do it. Coward.

Saunders: For convincing me that living in your basement while you were in university was the best idea ever. Also, for showing me that it is possible to get cheese stuck in your hair while eating a Pizza Pop.

Doni: For our lunches, heated debates, and heart-to-hearts. Thanks for always listening.

The Young Guns: For a million memories. Regulators, mount up.

Miss Ross: I would have written "Kat," but that's unnatural. You are forever Miss Ross. Thank you for being an amazing teacher and an incredible human being. Thanks for seeing potential.

Tuesday Basketball Buddies: D-up.

Doug: For never treating me like a punk kid, even when I was a punk kid.

Japan: For the adventures, the strange game shows, and changing my life.

Niall: For being a big bro in a land far away from my actual family.

Toby: For the adventures, random karaoke sessions, and showing me that I don't know anything about European capitals. Toby McTobyerson.

Colin: Thanks to you, I know that a relative clause isn't Santa's nephew.

Tom: For trusting me enough to let me borrow money from the store safe to get my visa to work in Japan.

Nobu: For the amazing food, classic camping trips, and great advice and insight.

CSI Annex: For giving me the space to write, create, and be inspired.

Joyce Scott: You might not know this, but you got the ball rolling for me. I am forever indebted. Thank you for your support and amazingly kind heart.

Grant Baldwin: Your goatee is perfection. You are a good dude who has helped me keep the speaking business on track.

Alton Jamison: Our phone calls kept things moving forward when times were tough.

Blake Fly: You are truly a brother from another mother. But not really. But kinda. But not really.

Michelle: This version of the book would literally never have happened if you didn't sit in my session at SXSWedu. Thank you.

Suzy: For putting up with my drawn-out stories, bad Wi-Fi connections, hectic travel schedule, Canadian English, and late deadlines.

The Students: For the thousands and thousands of emails you have sent me sharing your stories. You are why I do what I do. I am completely humbled by your courage, humor, and ability to play on your iPhone, text, play Xbox live, and watch YouTube fail videos at the same time. In your sleep. While writing a two-thousand-word essay on the importance of Anne Frank in modern-day society.

You: For having the courage to carve your own path and make your own lunch. Thank you for reading this book.

RESOURCES & TOOLS

Here's a collection of resources that may be helpful as you make some of the decisions talked about in this book.

Enjoy :)

Travel

www.couchsurfing.org – Awesome site to meet travel guides and travel buddies.

www.airbnb.com – Great local accommodations in just about every city around the world.

www.matadornetwork.com – Incredible site for travel inspiration.

www.hipmunk.com – Book your flight already!

www.mobissimo.com – Compare a ton of different flight options and prices.

www.flightfox.com – Have somebody else plan your travel.

Work

www.raiseyourflag.com – A site to find your career path and the companies that will hire you (P.S. this is my company).

www.themuse.com – Learn about some of the greatest companies to work for.

www.craigslist.com – If you don't know what this is, put the book down. There's something called the Internet you should see.

www.monster.com – Job postings.

Mentors

www.clarity.fm – Mentorship from experts.

www.micromentor.org – Mentors for entrepreneurs.

www.mentii.com – Career guidance from your future self.

Volunteering

www.idealist.org – Internships and volunteer opportunities around the world.

www.volunteermatch.org – Believe it or not, this site *matches* you with *volunteer* opportunities. They do it all based on what you care about.

www.volunteerhq.org – Gap-year programs and super affordable volunteering programs.

www.gooverseas.com – A ton of different travel, study, volunteer, and working opportunities around the globe.

HOW TO CONTACT ME

So, here's how it works: I personally respond to every email I get. I'm the only person that reads them, and I do everything I can to find the answers. If you ever have any questions or want to challenge me to a thumb war, it's on.

Hollerate.

Email: rporter@makeyourownlunch.com
Twitter: @lunch_buddy
Facebook: www.facebook.com/makeyourownlunch
Smoke Signal: 43.6426°N 79.3871°W

ABOUT RYAN

As a college student, Ryan Porter set out to answer the question, "What should I do with my life?" That question brought him to Tokyo, Japan, where he worked as an English teacher. The questions that followed continue to bring Ryan to different places around the globe.

From scuba diving in Honduras and surfing in Hawaii to backpacking through Europe and camping on active volcanoes in Guatemala, Ryan knows what it means to live life on his own terms.

He spends his working life helping teens to break free from conformity and create the exact future that they want to live through his *Make Your Own Lunch* live presentation, his company's software www.raiseyourflag.com, and this book.

For more information about Ryan, visit his website: www.ryanspeaks.com.